A SOUTH INDIAN TREATISE ON THE KAMASASTRA

THE RATI-RATNA-PRADIPIKA OF PRAUDHA-DEVARAJA MAHARAJA

A SOUTH INDIAN TREATISE ON THE KAMASASTRA

THE RATI-RATNA-PRADIPIKA OF PRAUDHA-DEVARAJA MAHARAJA

Swami Sivapriyananda

Preface by
Norman Sjoman

ABHINAV PUBLICATIONS

abhinav publications

First Published in India **2000**

Publishers
Shakti Malik
Abhinav Publications
E-37, Hauz Khas
New Delhi-110016 (INDIA)
Phones: 6566387, 6524658, 6562784
Fax: 91-11-6857009
e-mail: shakti@nde.vsnl.net.in
abhinav.abhinaf@axcess.net.in
Website: http//www.abhinavexports.com

ISBN 81-7017-388-4

Phototypesetting and processing by
Tara Chand Sons
Naraina, New Delhi

Printed at
D.K. Fine Art Press Pvt. Ltd.
Ashok Vihar, Delhi

CONTENTS

PREFACE

Sivapriyananda was in the midst of a rich period of scholastic contribution at the time of his unexpected and unfortunate demise. He was born in a royal family and became a repository of much of the learning and art that he was privileged to by birth. He completed a period of archeological studies and was fluent in at least nine languages. He had access to materials that are not on public display through different royal family connections. He had wandered throughout India as a samyasin on the circuits of the saints and samyasins and knew of cultural complexes that no one without that experience could have known. He published many small articles on curiosities that were singular and not in the established scholarly corpus like his work on the spit goddess. Unfortunately, no bibliography of his works has been compiled. His works are not of ready access as they have been published in minor magazines and other small publications that do not, as yet, come under any search system or indexing that would make it possible to compile a list of his extensive writing.

Rati-Ratna-Pradipika, although it is not complete and contains very little that is new in the field of erotica, was a particular interest to him because it was written by a member of the Wadiyar royal family to which he also belonged. He had completed the text which I managed to salvage from his computer. I have not touched the text or the notes except to make minor corrections.

Sivapriyananda had gotten some of the illustrations together for the text but he was not satisfied with those, hence the work was in abeyance. 'Ganjifa' Raghupati Bhatta, a very old friend of both myself and Sivapriyananda, an inspired master of erotica, supplied replications of some of his erotic ganjifa cards, many of which are illustrations of positions mentioned in this text. I have linked those that serve as some sort of description to the verses of the text. Raghupati Bhatta's art transcends the category of illustration. Therefore, I have included a body of work, some of which is drawn from the rich history of Indian erotica and thus coalesces with this text in many places although it actually serves as an individual aesthetic statement. Raghupati Bhatta's work here is not a replication of forms but an example of the spirit of the ancient masters of this art which enabled them, by inner vision, to bring their works of art into being.

It has given me great pleasure to bring this last work of my dear friend, Sivapriyananda and another scholarly article on Mysore drawing to the point of publication. I am sure that these last works will be received well by his many friends and colleagues for whom his loss is irreplaceable.

Mysore 1999

Dr. N.E. Sjoman
Editor

INTRODUCTION

To satisfy basic material needs for food, clothing, shelter and a decent life is artha (prosperity). Sexual pleasure and procreation is kama (pleasure). Moral laws, rituals and ethical values are dharma (righteousness). A longing to understand the mystery of life and the pursuit of spiritual enlightenment is moksha (liberation). These four, according to Indian tradition, are the fundamental aims of human life (purusartha) and need to be equally balanced and harmonized for happiness and fulfilment.

Ancient legend says that Prajapati, the lord of progeny, gave a long discourse on the first three aims of life. This discourse was in one hundred thousand lectures and contained guidelines for life on earth. From this vast fund of divine knowledge, Brhaspati, the teacher of the gods, selected instructions on material prosperity and composed his 'Arthasastra', which unfortunately is now lost to us in its original form. Manu, the law giver to the human race, took moral and ethical matters from Prajapati's discourse and compiled a treatise on dharma called 'Manusmrti'. Nandi, Siva's bull vehicle, collected all the relevant information on sexual pleasure and wrote a work on this subject. Nandi's work, however, was not merely theoretical. He carefully observed his master Siva and his beloved Parvati engaged in sexual play for a thousand years and codified this information into 1000 chapters. Many later writers on erotica quote opinions of one Nandikesvara—an expanded form of the name Nandi—and it is likely that this is a reference to a historical person. But no actual text, either by Nandi or Nandikesvara, is known.

Nandi's great work was still too voluminous for mortals to handle and so Svetaketu of the Uddalaka clan further reduced it to a more manageable work of 500 chapters.

The name of Svetaketu, son of Uddalaka Aruni, is known to us from Vedic literature (2150-1400 B.C.). According to references in the *Satapatha Brahmana* (XI.4.1-2) and the *Brhadaranyaka Upanisad* (VI.2) Svetaketu's father, Uddalaka Aruni, belonged to the Gautama gotra (lineage). He was a Brahmin of the priestly caste, an outstanding teacher of the Vedas and came from the Pancala area of northern India. Pancala of ancient India extended from the foothills of the Himalayas to the valley of the river Chambal. It was generally divided into north (uttara) and south (daksina) Pancala, separated by the Ganga river.

Svetaketu acquired all his father's learning but became proud and haughty. Full of pride he approached Pravahana Jaibali, the chief of Pancala. The chief was a learned philosopher and was aware of Svetaketu's arrogance and pride of scholarship. To reduce his false pride and test his knowledge he asked him five questions. The questions were metaphysical and Svetaketu could not answer them. Offended at his humiliation he rushed back to his father and demanded to know why he had failed to teach him metaphysical secrets. Aruni humbly admitted his ignorance and went to chief Pravahana Jaibali to learn the secret lore.

The metaphysical instructions given by Jaibali to Uddalaka Aruni included the mystery of sexual relationship and the sexual symbolism of Vedic rituals. He taught him that a woman was like the sacrificial fire. Her thighs were the offerings and her pubic hair the smoke that arises from the sacrificial altar. Her vagina was the heat of the fire and sexual intercourse the sparks that ignite it. Semen was the oblation that was offered into the sexual fire so that human beings can be born (*Brhadaranyaka Upanisad*, VI.2.13). Uddalaka Aruni also learnt the rules of approaching women for sex, dealing with wife's lovers and the secrets of obtaining good progeny.

Later, Uddalaka Aruni taught his son all that he had learnt from Pravahana Jaibali and Svetaketu became the first human authority on sexology and spread his knowledge in the

Pancala country [1] making it the seat of sex learning. Vatsyayana confirms Svetaketu's fame as an authority on erotica (*Kama-sutra*, I.1.9).

Svetaketu's lost work in 500 chapters was still too bulky for study and so Babhru and his descendants, the Babhravyas, reduced it further to a more manageable length of 150 chapters. The subject matter of the Babhravya treatise was grouped into seven sections: (1) General sexology (Sadharana), (2) Sexual union (Samprayoga), (3) Wooing unmarried girls (Kanya samprayukta), (4) Married life (Bharyadhikara), (5) Extramarital relations (Para-daraka), (6) Prostitution (Vesyadhikara) and (7) Aphrodisiacs, herbs and occult charms (Aupanisadika). The Babhravyas, like Svetaketu, were also from the Pancala area.

Later, between the third and first centuries B.C. many writers and scholars took parts of the Babhravya thesis and made specialized studies on each of the seven sections. Dattaka was the adopted son of a Brahmin woman and lived in ancient Pataliputra (modern Patna in the state of Bihar) the capital of Candragupta Maurya (320 B.C.). From very young age he wanted to fathom the ways of the world and chose to live in the company of courtesans. After an eventful life of learning he was requested by Virasena, one of the foremost courtesans of Pataliputra, to write his life experience down in a book. Dattaka obliged by synthesizing his learning with the material from Babhravya's sixth section on prostitutes compiling a treatise on courtesans. Dattaka's work is now lost to us but from the many references to it in later literature it is clear that it was once a very authoritative work on the subject. King Madhava Varman II (c 380 A.D.) of the Ganga dynasty wrote a summary of it, two chapters of which are still available. Damodaragupta (779-813 A.D.), who wrote on the guiles of prostitutes, mentions Dattaka in his *Kuttanimatam.*

Carayana or Dirgha-Carayana wrote a treatise on general sexology based on Babhravya's first section. Carayana is known to have been a minister of King Prasenajit of Kosala (country along the banks of the Sarayu river with its capital at Ayodhya) who was a contemporary of Lord Gautama Buddha (544-461 B.C.).

Suvarnanabha wrote on sexual union (second section of Babhravya), Ghotakamukha on wooing unmarried girls (third section of Babhravya), Gonardiya on married life (fourth section of Babhravya), Gonikaputra on extramarital sex (fifth section of Babhravya) and Kucumara on aphrodisiacs and occult charms (seventh section of Babhravya). Not much is known about Suvarnanabha, Ghotakamukha and Kucumara and their works are not available to us. But there are references to Gonardiya and Gonikaputra in Patanjali's (third century B.C.) grammatical commentary *Mahabhasya.* Gonardiya appears to have been a famous grammarian who lived at the time of Patanjali and Gonikaputra is probably another name for Patanjali himself (Abhyankar & Shukla, 1986, 144).

The renowned *Kama-sutra* of Vatsyayana Mallanaga is the first and earliest sex manual that has come down to us in more or less its original form. Vatsyayana, however, does not claim to be the first and narrates the long tradition of erotica (I.1.5-14) starting from the lord of progeny to the seven specialized monographs on Babhravya's thesis.

Vatsyayana says that the wave of specialization after Babhravya had adversely affected the study of Kama-sastra (erotica) in the Pancala region. Voluminous specialized works discouraged serious study of erotica as a whole and the ancient knowledge was in the danger of being lost. To save sexology and to synthesise it into a more convenient sized treatise Vatsyayana composed his sutras. Following tradition he divides his subject matter into the seven sections (adhikarana)—of general sexology, sexual union, wooing unmarried girls, married life, extramarital sex, courtesans and aphrodisiacs and charms, twenty-six chapters (adhyaya), sixty-four topics (prakarana) and one thousand two hundred and fifty sutras. Though Vatsyayana has followed the traditional arrangement for his work, it is not a repetitious reworking of old knowledge. It is an original and individual production that surpasses all later erotica. It is comprehensive, clear, open minded and discusses all relevant material connected with Kama-sastra known in his time.

The date of Vatsyayana's *Kama-sutra* is difficult to determine and ranges from fourth century B.C. to third century A.D. The short sutra style and the picture of society it represents probably suggests an early date, sometime between the fourth and third centuries B.C.

There are six commentaries of the *Kama-sutra* of which the *Jayamangala* by Yasodhara is the most comprehensive and well known. This commentary was written under the patronage of Chahamana king Visaladeva (1153-1163 A.D.). The celebrated scholar Ksemendra, student of the great Abhinavagupta and court poet of King Ananta (1029-1064 A.D.) of Kashmir, is said to have written a summary of Vatsyayana's work appropriately called '*Vatsyayana-sutra-sara*' (essence of Vatsyayana's sutras). This commentary however is lost. A commentary by Virabhadradeva is well known as an independent work called the *Kandarpacudamani* (tiara of love god). This is a very skilful and faithful reworking, in Arya metre, of the entire *Kama-sutra* and was probably ghost written by a court scholar for king Virabhadradeva (c 1577 A.D.), son of Ramacandradeva of the Vaghela dynasty of western India. There are two minor and less known commentaries, one is by Malladeva and other that is anonymous. A late commentary by Bhaskara Narasimha was written sometime at the end of the eighteenth century and is known as the Vatsyayana *sutra vrtti*.

A very fascinating, but unfortunately lost, work on erotica was the remarkable *Gunapataka* (standard of good qualities) by a notorious figure generally known to later Sanskrit literature as Muladeva, though he had many aliases such as Mulabhadra, Bhadra, Devadatta (given by the gods) and Karnisuta (son of Karni). The last name suggests that his mother's name was Karni, but his father's name is not known. He was a master in the dubious craft of thieving and an adapt in the art of enticing young women. He was the very 'personification of chicanery' (Upadhyaya, 1965, 3). Crooks, cheats, scoundrels, vagabonds and all types of villainous characters surrounded him day and night. He gave them all good advice and guidance and at night sat on a high pedestal to give well attended discourses on how to cheat, defraud, swindle and steal, his favourite criminal subjects. He is said to have collected a sizable fortune with the help of his special associates Vipula (plentiful), Acala (immovable), Sasi (moon-like) and Kandali. Muladeva was so charismatic that many young men wanted to become his students and acolytes. Ksemendra in his *Kala-vilasa* says that a wealthy merchant called Hiranyagupta (gold-protector) placed his young son Candragupta (moon-protector) in Muladeva's care to be trained and educated in the art of cheating. Like all gangsters, Muladeva loved women and two famous courtesans Devadatta (god-given) and Anangasena (Cupid's army) fought bitterly for his attention (*Jayamangala* commentary on *Kama-sutra* VI.1.17). But Muladeva admired an experienced courtesan named Gunapataka and he is said to have composed his work, of the same name, to immortalize her. Though the *Gunapataka* text is not available to us today it was probably written in the form of a dialogue between the author and his beloved courtesan Gunapataka. Muladeva's date is not known for certain, but as Dandin, the author of the classical Sanskrit prose romance *Dasakumaracarita*, mentions him by name—as 'Karnisuta'—he lived before the sixth century A.D.

Damodaragupta was the prime minister of king Jayapida Deva (779-813 A.D.) of the Karkota dynasty of Kashmir. He has left us a very interesting and unusual work called the *Kuttanimatam* (advice of a cunning prostitute) in which an old prostitute tells a young one how to win over and fleece weak minded rich young men. Though this is not strictly a work on erotica in the *Kama-sutra* tradition it does deal with some of the topics from the sixth section of Babhravya's original treatise.

Nagara-sarvasva (town dweller's companion) is a fine guide book for the cultured urbanite and covers such topics as kissing, sex magic and detection of faults in gems rather elaborately. Written by Padmasri or Padmasrijnana (about 10th century A.D.), who was probably a Buddhist monk as he invokes Tara and Manjusri, both Mahayana Buddhist deities, at the beginning of the work.

After the *Kama-sutra*, the *Rati-rahasya* (secrets of love) of Koka pandita is the most renowned sex manual. All that is known about the author is that his grandfather was known as Tejoka, his father was called Gadya-Vidyadhara Kavi, he came from a Kashmiri Brahmin family and was the protege of one Vainyadatta. Koka pandita is generally believed to have lived sometime between 830 and 960 A.D. There are four known commentaries on *Rati-rahasya*: (1) by Kancinatha, (2) Avantya Ramacandra, (3) Kavi Prabhu and (4) the *Srngara-rasabandhapradipika* by Harihara.

The *Pancasayaka* of Jyotirisvara Kavisekhara is an elegant little work written sometime in the fourteenth century A.D. It is divided into five sections called arrows (pancasayaka) of Cupid.

After the *Kama-sutra* and *Rati-rahasya*, the *Ananga Ranga* (stage of the love god) of Kalyana-malla is the most celebrated and popular erotic text. It has been translated into Arabic, Persian and Turkish languages where it is known as *Lizzat-al Nissa* (pleasures of women). According to the author himself (I.2-7) the work was composed for the delectation of prince Lad Khan, son of Ahmed Khan of the Lodi family. There has been no Lodi ruler named Ahmed Khan but it is possible that he was some minor nobleman. According to the historical work *Waki'at-ti Mushtaki* of Saikh Rizku-lla-Mushtaki an Ahmed Khan, son of Jumal Khan Lodi Sarang-Khani, was appointed the governor of Jaunpur during Sultan Sikandar II Lodi's time (1489-1517 A.D.). Lad Khan may have been one of his sons (Ray, 1964, 24).

Smaradipika (light of love) of Rudra is a collection of erotic poems different from the Pancala style of the *Kama-sutra*. It may have come from a different region, probably southern India, and may represent a divergent erotic tradition (Comfort, 1965, 84). The *Ratimanjari* (poesy of love) by Jayadeva is a charming little work in 125 verses similar in style to the *Smaradipika*. Very little is known about the author of this little work but he is definitely not the same as the renowned Jayadeva of the *Gita Govinda.*

DATE AND AUTHORSHIP OF RATI-RATNA-PRADIPIKA

According to the colophon at the end of each chapter, in both the printed editions consulted,[2] the authorship of the *Rati-ratna-pradipika* is attributed to Praudha Devaraja Maharaja. A Dodda (Kannada word for 'Praudha' meaning elder) Devaraja Wadiyar II is known to have been the ruler of Mysore from 1659 to 1673 A.D. As the manuscripts on which the Mysore edition is based came from the Mysore area the editor, Pandita K. Rangaswami Iyengar (1922, 1), presumed the author to have been the ruler of Mysore. Another reason for ascribing our text to the Mysore ruler is the mention of the title 'Raja-paramesvara' (lord of kings) in one of the manuscripts. This title was used by Dodda Devaraja Wadiyar II on ceremonial occasions (Iyengar, 1922, 1). Ray (1964, 22) however identifies the author of *Rati-ratna-pradipika* with Immadi (second) Praudha Devaraya (1422-1446 A.D.), the famous Sangama dynasty ruler of Vijayanagara.

Dodda Devaraja Wadiyar II was born on May 25, 1627 and came to the Mysore throne as the adopted son of Kanthirava Narasimharaja Wadiyar I (1638-1659 A.D.) on August 19, 1659. He was the third son of Muppina Devaraja and the grandson of Bettada Camaraja V who ruled for a very short period from 1576 to 1578 A.D. Devaraja was adopted only three days before king Kanthirava's death.

Devaraja II had two queens, Muddajamma and Devajamma. Though he was busy with many wars he was a great builder and the large monolithic stone Nandi bull halfway up Chamundi hills near Mysore was carved under his patronage. He is also known to have laid the 1001 stone steps that lead up to the temple and are still used by pilgrims. He was also a patron of literature and two well known poets, Tirumalacara and Camayya, adorned his court. However, apart from the probable authorship of our text no other work is attributed to him.

During his lifetime, the prefix 'Dodda' was not added to his name as his elder brother was known by that name. Only after his death was the prefix used to distinguish him from his nephew and successor Cikka (younger) Devaraja (Rao,1943, 267 and 544-545).

Immadi Praudha Devaraya formally came to the Vijayanagara throne in 1426 after the death of his father Vijayaraya, though he had been active in politics and administration a long time before his ascension. Immadi Devaraya was known as 'Gaja-betakara' (hunter of elephants) though it is not certain if the word 'gaja' or elephant refers to his strong enemies or to the actual animal. The Persian traveller Abdur Razzak, who came to Vijayanagara during Immadi Devaraya's rule, was much impressed by the king and his domain and said that his empire extended from Ceylon in the south to Gulbarga in the north and Orissa in the east to the Malabar coast in the west. The king was a learned poet and a patron of Sanskrit, Telugu and Kannada literature. He frequently presided over many literary disputations.

It is very difficult however to decide which of the two kings wrote our text, as both were scholars and patrons of literature and are likely candidates for its authorship.

NOTES

1. The Pancala school of Babhravya held that a woman lost her chastity status only if she had sex with more than five men (*Kama-sutra*, 1.5.30). The most famous classical example of a chaste woman with five husbands is Draupadi, wife of the five Pandava princes in the *Mahabharata* epic. Draupadi, also known as 'Pancali', belonged to the Pancala region. Some scholars have gone so far as to suggest that the sexual rites performed during the Asva-medha horse sacrifice originated in the Pancala region (De, 1969, 93).
2. The two printed editions consulted are (i) edited by Pandita K. Rangaswami Iyengar, published in 1922 from Mysore and (ii) as section 9 in the collection known as '*Kama-kunja-lata*', edited by Panditaraj Dhundhiraja Sastri, published in 1967 by Chowkhamba Sanskrit Series Office, Varanasi. The manuscript text published in this volume is of recent origin and probably written by a scribe from the Mysore area.

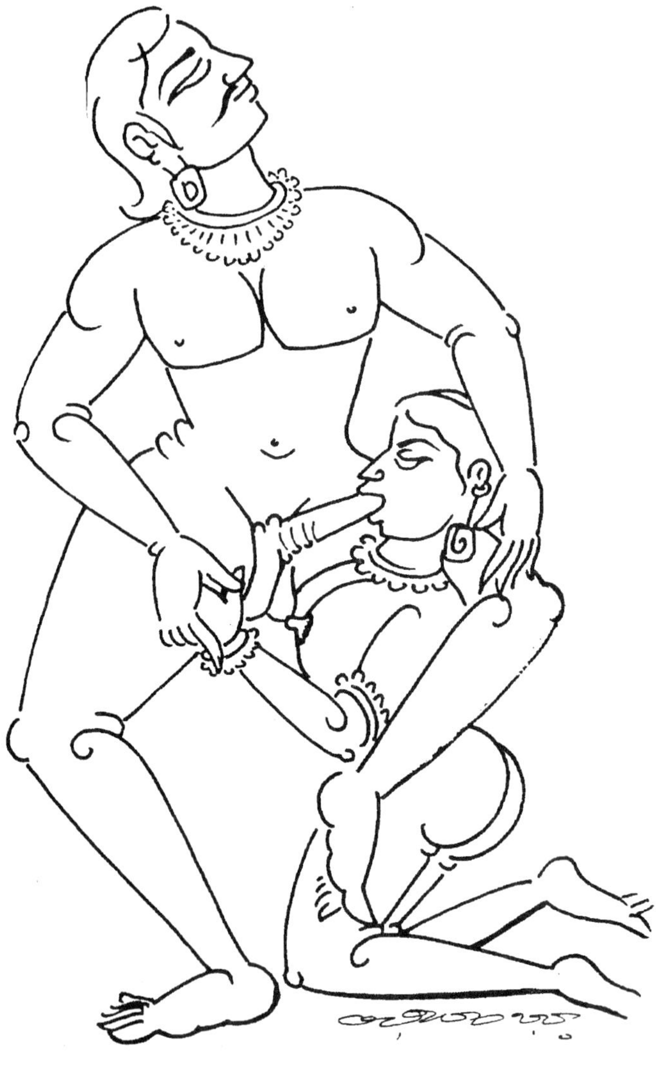

Vicitra

THE INFLUENCE OF THE PHASES OF THE MOON ON THE SEXUAL DESIRE OF WOMEN ACCORDING TO THE SYSTEM OF GAUNIPUTRA (GAUNIPUTRA-MATE SUKLA-KRSNAPAKSA-KRIDA-ADHIKARA)

First the physical classification of women (jati-nirdesa); then the qualities of a hero (nayaka laksana); then outer and inner love play (bahya-antara rati); then a section on one's own and other men's wives (sva-anya dara adhikara); and then, in proper order, a section on courtesans and prostitutes (varanari adhikara). (1-2a).

Though the beginning verses of the Sanskrit texts give a list of only five sections (adhikara), the printed text has seven sections. These however do not follow the order given in the introductory verses. The actual order in the printed (Iyengar, 1922) text is: (1) The influence of the phases of the moon on the sexual desire of women according to the system of Gauniputra (Gauniputra-mate sukla-krsnapaksa-krida-adhikara); (2) Types of women (Jati-vivarana); (3) Outer love play between men and women (Nayika-nayaka bahya surata); (4) Inner love play (Abhyantara-rati); (5) Postures of inner sex play (Abhyantara-ratau karana); (6) Superior or 'oral' sex (Auparistaka); and (7) All forms of love making (Sarva-surata). So, even though K. Rangaswami Iyengar, the editor of the text, says that "I have been able to bring out this edition of the whole work" (1922, p. 1), the printed Mysore version is far from complete. The existing work stops at all 'forms of love making'. The sections on one's own and other men's wives and on courtesans, which the author mentions in the first verse, are missing. It is possible that, being a practical manual, several versions of the work were in circulation and the manuscript material is mixed up.

Terms such as 'a body as soft as a lotus bud', 'vaginal secretions and body odour are like the perfume of lotus flowers', 'clitoris (love's parasol) that looks like the carpel of a budding lotus' and so on are terms used in classifying women. The fourfold classification suggested by Nandisa and Gauniputra is as follows: (2b-4).

That which is known by such fancy poetic terms as 'the love fluid' (smarodaka) or the 'sweat of the goddess of love' (Rati-sveda) is the liquid secreted from the vaginal walls, by the Bartholins glands, during sexual arousal. This acts as a natural lubricant to the movement of the penis. These secretions are very essential for smooth penetration during intercourse. Some women may not lubricate naturally in which case sexual enjoyment becomes difficult. This is the reason why writers on traditional Indian erotica recommend long and extended foreplay before intercourse.

The clitoris is a small bud of tissue at the front of the vulva. This is the exact counterpart of the male penis and is responsible for sexual arousal. It swells up and becomes hard, like the penis, on sexual stimulation.

Lotus-like woman (Padmini), woman of talent (Citrini), conch-shell like woman (Sankhini) and elephantine woman (Hastini). These are considered progressively less and less desirable. (5).

PADMINI

Eyes slightly red at the corners; gait like that of a goose; breasts like ripe coconuts; nose like the delicate sesame flower; respected by elders of society; complexion

either fair, like the camphor flower, or evenly dark like the blue lotus; sharp eyes like those of a gazelle pursued by hunters; three folds marking her belly; well dressed; demeanour like that of a swan; soft, meagre and clean diet; shy; dignified; a weakness for fair lower lips; full of passion on the second, third and fifth day of the lunar month; sexual desire aroused fully in the third quarter of the night and a liking for the lotus posture in intercourse: these are the qualities of a lotus-like woman. (6-10).

CITRINI

The characteristics of a woman of talent are: she is neither too tall nor too short; her body is lean and slender; she walks gracefully; her breasts and hips are fleshy but her shanks are thin; her voice is like that of a parrot; she has protruding lips and round conch-shell shaped neck; her love fluid is plentiful and smells of honey; she is usually an accomplished dancer and musician and has a flair for the fine arts; she loves external stimulation; her pubic region is soft and raised and is covered with very light hair; she has quick roving eyes; her sexual desire becomes intense during the first quarter of the day and night and on the sixth, eighth, tenth and twelfth day of the lunar month and enjoys intercourse in the 'urban' (nagarika) position. (11-15).

SANKHINI

A woman who adores blood red garlands and clothes; who is very quick and hot tempered; whose speech is indistinct; whose pubic region is covered with thick, shaggy hair; whose love fluid is pungent; who is thin and fair and eats in moderation; who likes to make profuse nail marks during intercourse; who is of bilious disposition and treacherous by nature; who becomes sexually aroused in the third watch of the day and night and on the eleventh and thirteenth day of the lunar month belongs to conch-shell class. (16-19).

HASTINI

An ungainly gait; corpulent and fleshy body; fickle mind; brownish hair; short stout neck; cruel, sadistic and shameless; throaty voice; love fluid as stringent, bitter and muddy as the secretions of a rutting elephant; large protruding lips; pubic region covered with minute fur-like hairs; gaping house of the love god (vagina); delight in rough sex; arousal during the third quarter of the day and night and on the fourth, seventh, ninth, fourteenth and fifteenth day of the lunar month; preference for the feet on shoulder coital posture; these qualities are that of an elephantine woman. (20-24).

The characteristics of the four classes of women described here are very broad and general. In practical life, to determine the class to which a woman belongs, one has to consider the sum total of all qualities. (25).

Attempts to classify men and women on the basis of their physical and mental traits go back a long way into human history. Though such classifications cannot be considered either very scientific or accurate many schemes have been put forward by philosophers, astrologers, sexologists, medical doctors and psychologists over the centuries. The Greek physicians Hippocrates (about 400 B.C.) divided human beings into two groups: phthisic (wasting) and apoplectic (struck). Phthisic people were understood to be thin and tall with a tendency towards diseases such as tuberculosis. Apoplectic were said to be big-made, heavy and fat and usually susceptible to heart ailments. Ayurvedic system of Indian medicine classified human beings into three categories based either on quality (guna)—sattva (equilibrium), rajas (activity) and tamas (inertia) or nature (prakrti)—vata (wind), pitta (bile) and kapha (phlegm). More recent (1940s) characterization of men is suggested by the psychiatrist William Sheldon (1898-1970). He isolated three primary physical or somato types: endomorphic, ectomorphic and mesomorphic. The endomorphs tend to be round, soft and fat with very small penises, sometimes completely hidden in the pubic hair. Ectomorphs are thin, fragile and delicate with genitals that appear to be large in comparison to the rest of the body. The middle mesomorphs are muscular, athletic, square and hard with well developed (whatever that means!) penises and thick and firm scrotums. Temperamentally, endomorphic people love comfort, are sociable and like to eat much (viscerotonia). Ectomorphic people like physical adventures and action (somatotonia) while mesomorphics are inhibited and restrained (cerebrotonia). The sexual interests of Sheldon's three somatotypes are also said to differ. Endomorphics tend to go in more for friendship and companionship than actual physical sex. Ectomorphics have an intense sex drive. Mesomorphics like physical sex but are very matter of fact about it and lack much imagination (Sheldon et al., 1954). Like many other human typologies Sheldon's deals primarily with males. Other modern classifications include those of analytical psychologist Carl Jung (1875-1961) and behavioural psychologist Hans Eysenck (born 1916). Jung divided human beings into extroverts, who tend to be out-going and sociable, and their diametrically opposite introverts. Eysenck developed and altered this further into a fourfold classification: (1) extroverted-unstable or the warrior; (2) introverted-unstable or the recluse; (3) extroverted-stable or the ruler; and (4) introverted-stable or the philosopher. However, it should be made clear that from my point of view all attempts at standardizing men and women into classes can be neither accurate nor cover the vast variety of human beings on this planet. It is simply an intellectual exercise (see Gregersen, 1982 and Walker, 1977).

Sexual Calendar (kama-kala)

Now to consider the seats of passion according to the waxing and waning of the moon. During the bright half of the lunar month a woman's passion-centre moves upward from left toe to the top of the head. In the dark half of the lunar month the erogenous spots on a woman's body descend from the head to the toe on the right side of the body. (26-27).

On the first day of the bright half press her toe with your toe.

On the second day press her foot with your foot. On the third day touch her ankles with your ankles. On the fourth day rub against her thighs with your thighs. On the fifth day play the elephant trunk game with your fingers in her vagina. On the sixth day massage her navel with your palm. On the seventh day smack her breasts with your fist. On the eighth day playfully rub her breasts. On the ninth day make nail marks in her armpit. On the tenth day mark her neck with your nails. On the eleventh day kiss her cheeks again and again. On the twelfth day press her mouth with your lips and teeth. On the thirteenth day kiss her eyelids gently. On the fourteenth day slap and kiss her forehead. On the fifteenth day pull her hair. Women can do the same things to the right side of the man's body during the bright half of the lunar month. (28-35).

In traditional erotica, many methods of stimulating the yoni (the clitoris and the vagina) are described. Ray (1964, p. 58) mentions the names of some of these and says that these were recommended by ancient authors so that women can achieve orgasm at the same time as the man. He calls them Angulipravesa (finger-entry) and gives a list of descriptive names: karikara-krida (elephant trunk game), phanibhoga (serpent's hood), kamankusa (Cupid's goad), pravesana (entry), kanaka (golden), pataka (banner), trisula (trident), kamayudha (Cupid's weapon), kamausadha (love's medicine) and Manmatha-pataka (Cupid's flag). Three fingers—ring, middle and index—together form the elephant trunk gesture (karikara-mudra). Tickling the yoni with fingers held in this gesture is the elephant trunk game.

During the dark half of the lunar month sites of Cupid (erogenous zones) on a woman's body should be stimulated in the reverse order. Titillation of these zones makes the woman wet with joy. (36).

When a man looks at his beloved, his passionate sight should fall on her heart, breasts, eyes, head and the hidden

place, like the five powerful burning arrows released from the bow of Cupid; arrows that cause a sea of sensual doom like the one let loose at the end of time by Siva, enemy of the love god. (37-39).

Kamadeva, the ancient Indian god of love and sexual desire is very much like Eros and Cupid. Eros, the Greek god of love, is said to have been born from the union of Heaven and Earth. He is represented as a young man who awakens love in the hearts of gods and humans with the help of his bow and arrow. Cupid, the Roman counterpart of Eros, is depicted as a winged youth holding a bow and arrow. He is the son of the planetary deities Mars and Venus. The Indian love god Kamadeva is also represented as a young, handsome man with a bow and five arrows. His bow is the stalk of fresh sugarcane and his arrows are of five different flowers: aravinda (lotus), asoka (Saraca indica), cuta (mango), navamallika (jasmine) and nilotpala (blue lotus). These arrows have symbolic names that stand for the emotional states that one experiences in young love: unmada (excitement), tapana (burning), sosana (desiccation), stambhana (cessation of all activity) and sammoha (intoxication). Kamadeva rides on a parrot, the symbol of spring. He has many consorts but the chief among them is Rati (love). Kamadeva is known by names that either describe his effect on human sexuality or his iconographic form. Some of most commonly used epithets are Manmatha (mind agitator), Manobhu and Manasija (mind born), Madana (passion), Puspa-dhanva (one with floral arrows), Pancasayaka (holder of five arrows), Kusumayudha (one who has floral weapons), Minaketana (one whose banner is marked with a fish) and the most interesting of all 'Kandarpa' (whom should I inflame?, a question he is supposed to have asked at birth of his creator Brahma). According to the *Siva-purana* (Sati khanda) Brahma sent Kamadeva to disturb Siva's penance, awaken passion in him and divert his mind to Parvati so that Siva would marry her and get a son who would destroy a fierce demon called Tarakasura. At first Kamadeva succeeded in disturbing Siva and awakening his dormant libido. But unfortunately Kamadeva became the victim of Siva's cosmic anger which not only burnt the god of love to ashes but also started a universal catastrophe (Rao, 1989).

In the opinion of Gaunikaputra women are of four kinds. Now, a discussion about that which is special about the erogenous zones and their relation to the phases of the moon (kama-kala). (40).

During the dark half of the lunar month sexually sensitive sites on a woman's body move down in the following order: head, breasts, hands, nipples, thighs, navel, house of love (vagina), forehead, the three folds on the belly, buttocks, armpits, neck, hips and arms. Beginning from the first day of the bright half of the lunar month the erogenous zones move upward. (41-43a).

Now imagine that these fourteen stations of the love god are the fourteen vowels, including the aspirate (visarga). And each is nasalized with the addition of the dot (bindu). These are the sites to be stimulated to excite her and make her lubricate. Beginning with the first lunar day and taking one vowel for each day the lover should arouse her at the appropriate sites. (43b-45).

Here is an interesting instance of punning by using terms from grammar to convey erotic meaning. There are thirteen vowels (svaras) in the Sanskrit phonetic alphabet. These are: five simple vowels a, i, u, r, lr; four diphthongs e, ai, o, au; and four long varieties, aa, ii, uu, and rr, of the simple vowels. Added together we have a total of thirteen vowel sounds. Add the aspirate sound of visarga and the total comes up to fourteen. A nasal sound (anu-svara = that which is pronounced after a vowel) is added to vowels and consonants in the formation of words. Technically it is not a pure vowel but in writing it is generally represented as a 'dot' or bindu. Our author here has punned on the words 'bindu'—which means both the nasal dot and semen and 'visarga'—meaning both the aspirate sound and ejaculation. The use of grammatical terms for sexual symbolism is not entirely new in Sanskrit literature and

Abhyankar and Shukla (1986, p. 2) quote an interesting example. Visarga is generally written as two dots or circles one above the other. Durgasimha sees this as a graphic symbol of a woman's breasts ('*Katantra-sutra-vrtti*', I, 1, 16).

On the first day of the lunar month playfully sniff the upper part of her body and press her neck. Later nibble at her lips and kiss her cheeks. Thrill her back and give her goose-pimple. Gently make nail marks on her body uttering the erotic 'sit' sound. (46-47).

The erotic 'sit' sound is produced by drawing air between closed teeth. The different varieties of love sounds are discussed in the seventh chapter of this work.

On the second day massage her breasts and kiss her cheeks and lips. Scratch and leave nail marks on her neck, eye-lids and nipples. Then embrace her tightly. (48-49a).

The third day should begin with a tight embrace. Make goose-flesh in her armpits and on her buttocks by gently scratching with nails. Embrace her again and kiss her lips making the 'sit' sound. The man who knows the art of love should then leave nail marks, known as 'churita', on her breasts. (49b-51a).

Nail marking is given in the third chapter of this work.

On the fourth day of the lunar month embrace and massage her breasts. Bite her lower lip and make nail grooves on her left breast. Mark her armpits with the 'churita' nail mark, and if the man is clever he can lie on top of her. (51b-52).

For the fifth day hold her hair by the left hand and bite her lips. Stroke her nipples so that her hair stand on end. Then kiss her breasts with a great show of pleasure. (53-54a).

On the sixth give her a tight embrace and bite her lips. Make light 'churita' marks on her navel and deep nail marks on her thighs. Then a man who knows the science of desire should make his own arousal very obvious to her. (54b-55).

Start the seventh day by titillating her house of the love

god with fingers held in the elephant trunk manner. Then kiss her lips and put love marks on her throat, cheeks and breasts. Embrace her firmly. (56-57a).

On the eighth day of the lunar month caress her neck and make the 'churita' nail mark on her navel. Then kiss the area around her lips and squeeze her breasts. (57b-58a).

Make 'churita' nail marks on her 'mount of Venus' so that her pubic hair stands on end, on the ninth day of the lunar month. Then play the elephant trunk game in her secret chamber. The knower of erotica can then bite her lips and scratch her back with nails. (58b-59).

On the tenth day kiss her forehead and make nail marks on her neck. Then fondle and press her breasts with the left hand. Tickle her vagina in the elephant trunk game. (60-61).

The eleventh day is for marking her neck with nail marks and cuddling her firmly. Then kiss her lips and pummel her breasts with the fist. The master of love play should then stroke her vagina in the elephant trunk manner. (62-63a).

The twelfth day of the lunar month starts with repeated kisses on her cheeks. Then cover her eyes and suck her lower lip while making the 'sit' sound. (63b-64a).

On the thirteenth day kiss her face and cheeks making the 'sit' sound. Pummel her breasts and make nail marks on her neck. (64b-65).

On the fourteenth day kiss her eyes and make goose-flesh in her armpits. First fondle her breasts and then the knower of love should play the elephant trunk game in her vagina. (65b-66).

On the festival of the full moon mark her neck again and again with nail marks. Caress her tightly and excite her vagina with the arrow of love. (67).

Arrow of love probably refers to the erect penis.

Arousing a woman in the proper way on the appropriate days of the lunar calendar will make her wet with passion. This

is the opinion of Gauniputra. Now let us look at Vatsyayana's theories. (68).

Thus ends the first chapter on the influences of the phases of the moon on the sexual desire of women according to Gauniputra in the work called 'Rati-ratna-pradipika' by King Devaraja the Elder.

Trivikramabhagavimardana

DESCRIPTION OF CLASSES (JATI VIVARANA)

Men and women can be divided into three classes on the basis of the length and depth of their respective genitals. (1).

Female sexual organs consist of the external vulva and the inner vagina. The vulva includes a pair of lips, the labia majora which cover and protect the more delicate inner lips known as the labia minora. At the front of the entrance to the vagina is a bud of erectile tissue called the clitoris. This is well supplied with nerves making it the most sensitive part of the female genitalia. One could say that the clitoris plays the most central role in sexual arousal and probably contributes more to enjoyment that the coitus itself. It is most aptly called the 'Cupid's parasol' (Kama-atapatra) in traditional Indian erotic literature.

Opening from the vulva is the short tube called the vagina. This tube is lined with mucus membrane which lubricates the delicate tissue and provides a suitable environment for the male sperm to survive on its journey to the unfertilized egg. The vagina is separated from the vulva by the thin piece of membrane known as the hymen. This is said to break at first penetration and is a sign of virginity. However this folklore idea is not entirely true. So many things can tear a hymen; it can be easily stretched or pushed aside even by using internal sanitary towels. The uterus or womb is joined to the top of the vaginal tube through a narrow channel called the cervix. The pair of ovaries are joined to the uterus by the Fallopian tubes, one on each side. The Fallopian tubes transport the unfertilized egg cells as they are released from the ovaries.

The male penis is a tube that serves the dual function of urination and delivery of sperm at the time of sexual intercourse. The tip of the penis is a sensitive portion called the glans. This, like the female clitoris, is well supplied with nerves and is the chief source of pleasurable sensation during sexual arousal. When not circumcised, the glans is covered with prepuce or foreskin. Inside the penis are three areas of soft spongy tissue which fill up with blood causing the penis to swell and become erect. Through the length of the shaft runs the urethral tube which conducts urine from the bladder as well as the sperm produced in the testicles. Inside the testicles are fine tubes coiled tightly and held hanging outside the body in a flexible sac called the scrotum. The testicles produce sperm at the rate of 200 million or more each day.

There is much myth and fantasy surrounding the size of the penis and the depth of the vagina. In actual fact the length of the penis is tremendously variable, ranging from four centimetres to twenty-one centimetres in the flaccid state. This variation can be seen even in individuals from the same racial, social and family backgrounds. Physiologically the size of the penis has no importance or consequence. The female vagina is about ten centimetres in depth but is capable of stretching to accommodate a baby or any size of penis (Ward, 1984).

The three classes of women are: gazelle (mrgi), mare (vadava) and elephant (hastini). Men also belong to three classes: hare (sasa), bull (vrsa) and horse (asva). Their characteristics, in order: (2)

A proportionate body; glossy, dark, curly and thick hair; narrow waist; delicate, even and firm teeth; small nose and nostrils; lotus eyes; proud; slim, delicate arms; rosy lips, palms and soles; long ears, neck and forehead; hidden ankles; fleshy, firm thighs; gait like an intoxicated elephant; glistening skin; quick mind; hot temper; clever in love play; moderate diet; love fluid the smell of flowers; straight, long and even fingers; guileless; amorous but lazy; gregarious; soft spoken and with

a vagina that is six fingers deep: these are the qualities of a doe-eyed gazelle woman. (3-8a).

A woman of the mare class has a head that leans slightly forward; eyes that look like lotus buds; straight, firm and dense hair; large breasts; thick, long face, temples and teeth; even fleshy arms; enormous lips; slender belly; soft lotus-like palms; ample breasts; deep honey bee-like voice; envious nature; lethargic disposition; deep navel; attractive appearance; tortuous hips and small thighs; broad waist; slight stoop on account of the heavy breasts; sluggish gait; fickle mind; clear speech; soft but dirty body; love for food, sleep and men; satisfied quickly in sex; determined mind; has plenty of love fluid that smells of sour curds; and a vagina that is nine finger breadth deep. (8b-14).

The characteristics of an elephant woman are: wide and drooping cheeks, ears and temples; short and fat ankles and arms; secretive and evil mind; slightly bent, short, fleshy neck; protruding teeth; compact dark hair; deep voice like that of an elephant; ever ready for sex; rough skin; big breasts and lips; very passionate disposition; low and reddish eyes; elephant ichor-like love secretions; love for rivers; sadistic nature; and a house of the love god twelve fingers deep. (15-19a).

A man of the hare class has large eyes that are slightly reddish; teeth that are small and even; round face; long, thin, soft and shining hair; well built arms and long fingers; pink palms and ankles; soft fingers that cling together; cultured speech; long neck and arms; amiable nature; straight shanks; small appetite; mildly passionate and not very keen on sexual satisfaction; lucky; respectable; ejaculates quickly but has semen that is thick and plentiful; his penis is six finger breadths long. (19b-23a).

Broad teeth and forehead; big face; fleshy ears; muscular neck; round tortoise-like torso; wide, strong and swollen chest; red ankles and palms; eyes that are like red lotuses with steady long eyelashes; swinging, playful gait; energetic disposition; soft speech; capable of enduring pain; slightly corpulent;

powerful but given to sleeping a lot; shameless when excited; phlegmatic; pungent body odour; fleshy body; much loved by women and a penis nine fingers long: these are, according to scholars, the characteristics of a bull man. (23b-28a).

A man of the horse class has lean and long ears, face, head, teeth and lips. His hair is thick and soft and his armpits are padded with fat. He can become fiercely jealous. His shanks are tortuous and his fingers, fingernails and eyes are elongated. He is mature but given to sleep and laziness. His voice is soft, deep and sweet and he is well spoken. He walks very fast and has muscular thighs. He is ablaze with desire and loves sensual pleasures. He ejaculates a lot of yellowish and pungent smelling semen. His penis is twelve finger breadths long. (28b-32a).

This classification of men and women on the basis of genital size can apply even to those who do not conform to absolute standards. The hare-gazelle classification has many intermediate types that show all (uttama), half (madhya) or very few (adhama) standard characteristics. In all classifications many individuals may differ from the standard. A wise scholar should understand classification basis of the largest number of common traits. (32b-34a).

Vatsyayana has described the various possible combinations for sexual intercourse between individual men and women of the various classes.

Ideally the lotus woman should unite with the hare man. The woman of talent and the conch-shell woman should have sexual intercourse with the bull man. The elephant woman should copulate with the horse man. (34b-35).

There has been a little misapplication here. After specifying attributes for the gazelle and hare classes the author has given pairing between the three classes of hare-bull-horse men and the earlier fourfold classification of Gauniputra. The pairing between the threefold genital size groups is described in the fourth section, just before sexual postures.

Now, according to the work known as *Gunapataka*, women can be flaccid (slatha), not too flaccid and not too firm or middling (madhya) and firm (ghana). (36).

Slim, dark, with a low waist and long separated from her lover: these are the basic attributes of a flaccid woman. (37).

The five traits of a firm woman are: fat, fair, short, high waist and always ready for sex. Those with mixed features are called middling. (38).

The flaccid and firm types of women can be further divided into seven categories based on age. At eight she is a virgin (kanya), at nine she becomes a virgin who has just started menstruating (rohini). At ten she is the fair maid (gauri). She is a girl (bala) until the age of sixteen. From the sixteenth to the thirtieth year she is known a youth (taruni). From thirty to fifty she is known as mature (praudha). After that she is an old woman (vrddha). (39-41a).

There is an obvious error here. According to all other texts she is a maid (gauri) at nine and the virgin who has just started menstruating (rohini) at ten.

Now, the methods of seducing women belonging to different age groups. A fair maid can be won over with fruits such as bananas, bread fruit, and mangoes. A girl can be allured with fragrant flowers, betel nuts and camphor-like perfumes. A virgin who has just started menstruating can be wooed with betel nuts, garlands, gentle embraces and kisses. A youth can be easily attracted with gifts of ornaments and clothes and petting (outer love play). A mature woman likes imaginative intercourse and sadistic games. An old woman can be approached through her children and grandchildren or sweet conversations about domestic and religious matters. (41b-45a).

There is another obvious error here in the text. The methods of seducing a girl (bala) and a virgin who has just started menstruating (rohini) have been interchanged. I have however corrected the text before translating.

The flaccid woman likes petting and foreplay while the firm woman prefers active coitus. The middling woman likes both, petting and intercourse. It is said by scholars of erotica that a young girl is pleased with petting, a mature woman with copulation and an old woman with imaginative sex play. (45b-47a).

Now we come to the three temperaments of the different classes of men and women. They are: phlegmatic (slesmala), bilious (pittala) and flatulent (vatala). (47b-48a).

Body joints and ankles of a phlegmatic woman are hidden by fat. She is proud but soft spoken. Her teeth, eyes and nails are shining. She is reliable in love and very gentle. Her house of the love god is deep, cold and fleshy. She has a small appetite and little thirst but she is frequently troubled by heat. Her arms are long. She is pure, truthful and clever. She has a fancy for hare's testicles, lotuses, gold and yellow orpiment. She is tall, dark and has thick black hair. She is good at friendly conversations. She is secretive and spiteful. Her voice resembles the call of a goose and cuckoo. She walks like a goose and is far sighted. Though she eats little she has a soft corner for astringent, bitter, dry, hot and spicy food. She has large eyes that are slightly red at corners and have tender eyelashes. She is loyal, honourable and modest. She is always drowsy. She generally sees lotuses, flying birds, cranes, geese, demons, angels, gods such as Indra and Varuna, egrets, horses and elephants in her dreams. (48b-55).

Prominent joints and ankles; fair complexion; warm body; ample and pale breasts; reddish eyes, nails and soles of the feet; black or tawny hair; tremendous thirst and appetite; a liking for ointments, ornaments and garlands; guileless, cheerful, intelligent and adventurous; a predilection for cold and a dislike for hot things; an oblique gait; saline sweat; low libido and quick satisfaction in sex; rough, warm and slack vagina; fondness for white clothes; fickle mind; heavy and flaccid body and limbs; partiality for astringent, spicy, sweet, cold and sour food; dream visions of great conflagration,

meteors, palasa (Butea frondosa) trees, and the pericarp of lotuses; short eyelashes, red, cool and attractive eyes; a very lazy disposition: these are some of the attributes of a bilious woman. (56-62a).

A woman of flatulent nature is infatuated by the company of men and talks about nothing else. Her body is firm. Her complexion, eyes and nails are dark. Her hair looks like a frayed feather. Her house of love is as rough as a cow's tongue. She has a lot of faults. She does not like anything cold. Her mind and memory are fickle. However, she looks upon all with genuine affection and has sympathy for the weak and poor. Her phlegm and bile are very low. She sleeps very little. Her voice is tremulous and tormented and she always has a wet runny nose. She passes her time dancing, joking, hunting, and singing. She relishes meat, sweets, sour and bitter things. She is thin, tall and walks slowly. She is difficult to understand but she is both fertile and loyal to her lover. She dreams of mountains, plains, clouds, elephant rides, flying, dogs, jackals, camels, cows, vultures and many other birds. She is frequently very lucky. (62b-69a).

Visual imagery that we experience during sleep is known as dreams. According to modern sleep research an average person starts dreaming about an hour after falling into deep, non-dreaming sleep. After this, we generally dream every ninety minutes, each dream phase lasting from ten to thirty minutes. The dream period is recognized by rapid eye movement referred to as REM sleep. Other physiological changes also take place during this dream period. The brain becomes more active, the pulse rate becomes less regular than during deep sleep, blood pressure changes and there is quick shallow breathing. However, the part of the brain known as pons inhibits muscle movement during dreams to prevent our bodies from moving and actually acting out our dreams. Just as deep sleep is essential for physical growth and well-being, dreams are indispensable for mental development.

Though there has been much academic research on dreams they are not properly understood. There are many theories ranging from those that claim dreams to be of purely physical origin (Thomas Hobbs 1588-1679) to those of Sigmund Freud (1865-1939) who concluded that dreams were expressions of repressed sexual frustrations. None of the so-called scientific theories proposed so far satisfactorily explain the mysterious phenomena of dreaming.

According to occult and spiritual beliefs dreams arise when the ego barriers of waking consciousness are lowered and perception goes beyond rational boundaries. Dreams can be experiences of the subtle or etheric body (suksma or linga sarira) on an astral plane. Dreams can be symbolic and can foretell coming events as when princess Mayadevi dreamt of a white divine elephant entering her womb before the birth of Gautama Buddha. Dreams of flying can symbolize spiritual freedom. There have been many instances where great saints and prophets have been initiated into divine knowledge or received divine revelations through dreams. According to Vyasa's *Yoga-bhasya* (on sutra III, 22), the oldest (probably 4th century A.D.) commentary on the *Yoga-sutras* of Patanjali dreams are a source of omens (arista). These omens can be of three kinds: those generated by oneself (adhyatmika), those that come from outside sources (adhibhautika) and those that are inspired by divine beings (adhidaivika). The dreams that men and women of the 'temperament' classification see probably refer to the concept of dreams being a source of good or bad omens. On the other hand, it is also possible that the author of our text has the ideas of the two well known Indian physicians Caraka and Susruta (both about 1st century B.C.) in mind. Caraka and Susruta believed that dreams symbolism can help in the diagnosis of diseases.

There are women who have mixed traits and natures. As these do not fall into any clearly defined class one should determine their nature on the basis of the largest number of common characteristics. (69b-70a).

Women can be further divided on the basis of their inner dispositions (sattva bheda). These overlap the traits of all the other classes. (70b).

A clean fragrant body, smiling serene face, prosperous with a lot of friends and servants, peaceful and unsullied intellect, religious and devotional: these are the attributes of women of divine disposition (deva-sattva). (71-72a).

Women of human disposition (nara-sattva) are kind hearted and gifted. They love to entertain guests. They are inclined towards religious matters and like to fast and make vows. (72b-73a).

Women who are fair, have a wanderlust, are lazy but get very agitated sleep during which they sigh and yawn a lot, and have a body odour of coconuts are known to belong to the snake disposition (naga-sattva). (73b-74).

According to sage Vatsyayana, women of nature-spirit disposition (yaksa-sattva) are shameless and have a predilection for drunken parties, and picnics in gardens, on hills and near lakes. They are hot tempered but love sexual intercourse. They are passionate and given to offering sacrifices to please deities. (75-76a).

Women of heavenly-being disposition (gandharva-sattva) are calm, generous and charming. They wear bright garments and enjoy perfumes and flowers. They are usually skilled in music, dancing, singing and hunting. (76b 77).

Plain erect body, undignified behaviour, fondness for intoxicating drinks and flesh, given to futile laughter, inclined to magical offerings at cross-roads: these are the qualities of women who belong to the devilish disposition (paisaca-sattva). (78-79a).

The wise men say that women whose eyes roll from side to side; who are always hungry and unsteady of mind; who like high places and enjoy secret coitus; who are obstinate, far-sighted and have a habit of hoarding are of the crow disposition (kaka-sattva). (79b-81a).

Wandering eyes, partiality for biting and scratching, fickle mind, love for jumping and climbing, cantankerous , weakness for sweet fruits of all kinds, thin body and timid nature belong to the poetic disposition (kavi-sattva). (81b-83a).

Women of donkey-like disposition (khara-sattva) are rude and use rough language. They are sadistic and prefer the company of rogues. They have tremendous endurance and eat anything that comes their way but are rarely satisfied. (83b-84).

Women of demonic disposition (raksa-sattva) are violent, fearless and have a hatred for learned men, elders and divine beings. They are partial to meat and wine and have cruel red eyes. (85-86a).

Accomplished in many branches of learning, intelligent and full of enthusiasm, firm mind, but harsh speech and a dislike for divine beings: these are the characteristics of anti-god-like disposition (danava-sattva). (86b-87).

Women who eat a lot, are strong and arrogant, walk as if intoxicated, have small half-closed eyes, are gluttonous and bad tempered but dignified, are of the elephant disposition (gaja-sattva). (88-89a).

There are many such dispositions, but afraid of making this work too long, end here. (89b).

Thus ends the chapter on the description of classes in the work called 'Rati-ratna-pradipika' by King Devaraja Maharaja the Elder.

Sangara

Parasparauparistaka

OUTER PLAY BETWEEN THE HERO (NAYAKA) AND HIS HEROINE (NAYIKA): (NAYIKA-NAYAKAYOH BAHYA-SURATA-NIRUPANA)

Now a consideration of outer love play according to traditional texts as well as the author's own understanding. Methods of erotic titillation, such as passionate gazes, are known as 'outer love play'. These include passionate gazing, embracing, kissing, scratching, biting and playing the elephant trunk game. All these can be used to sexually stimulate a woman. It is the firm opinion (of the elders) that 'outer love' is the prelude to the sexual act and that a man must excite his female partner to a point where she becomes moist with desire. (1-4a).

Foreplay is mutual body contact and stimulation that happens before actual sexual intercourse. It enhances the level of sexual arousal and leads to a more intense and satisfying sexual relationship. Foreplay is generally a continuous process which begins with mutual attraction and ends with coitus. At first, there is an increasing degree of both physical and emotional contact which involves holding hands, whispering loving words, kissing, embracing, biting, scratching and genital stimulation with the tongue and fingers. To begin with, easily accessible and open areas of the body, such as hands, face, lips, ears, neck, legs and buttocks are stroked. Then the breasts and nipples are pressed and fondled. These areas of the body are known as secondary erogenous zones because, though they are not directly involved in sexual intercourse, they are sensitive to touch and can lead to sexual arousal.

When foreplay becomes very intense it leads to genital stimulation. The genitals are considered to be the primary erogenous zones and include, in men, the penis, scrotum and the perineum (the area between the back of the scrotum and the anus), and the pubic region or mons veneris, the outer and inner lips of the vagina, the clitoris and the female perineum in women.

EMBRACING (ALINGANA)

There are twelve ways of embracing. Of these four are pleasurable before and eight during courtship. The eight embraces recommended during courtship are clinging like a creeper (lata-vestanaka), climbing a tree (vrksadhirudha), sesame and rice (tila-tandula), milk and water (ksira-nira), encircling the thighs (uru-upaguhaka), enclosing the waist (jangha-upaguhaka), caressing the breasts (stanalingana) and clasping the forehead (lalatikam). Embraces that are enjoyable before courtship are piercing (viddhaka), touching (sprstaka), rubbing (udghrstaka) and squeezing (pidita). (4b-7).

A woman approaches her lover with the intention of starting love play. She sportingly clings to him like a creeper caresses a tree. She then brings his face closer to her mouth and kisses him with the 'sit' sound. This is known as the 'clinging like a creeper' embrace. (8-9).

She puts her first step on his foot and the second one on his thigh. She embraces him with one arm behind his back, and attempts to climb him by placing the other hand on his shoulder. She then kisses him with the 'sit' sound. This is the 'climbing a tree" embrace which is best done while the man is standing. (10-12).

When the couple lie on a bed and hold each other tightly in their arms, it becomes the 'sesame and rice' embrace. (13).

A couple sit facing each other either on a bed or one lover on the lap of the other. They are both incited by passion and

hug each other so tightly that it looks as if they are trying to enter each other in a 'milk and water' embrace. (14-15a).

When a sexually excited lover caresses and squeezes his beloved's thighs with his own thighs it is called the 'encircling the thighs' embrace. (15b-16).

A woman, who is so fired by passion that her clothes have fallen away and her braided hair has become dishevelled, slowly mounts her supine lover with the excuse of kissing him. Instead she firmly holds his pubic region between her thighs. This is the 'enclosing the waist' embrace. (17-18).

Similarly, if a woman who has mounted her supine lover presses her breasts against his chest it becomes the 'caressing the breasts' embrace. (19).

When a lustful woman, lying on top of her lover, presses her mouth against his mouth, her eyes against his eyes and her forehead against his forehead it becomes the 'clasping the forehead' embrace. (20-21a).

On a formal occasion, when a man and woman are walking close to each other and their bodies happen to touch, this is the 'touching' embrace. (21b-22a).

To find out what is in the mind of the man she fancies, she makes an excuse to rub her breasts against him while his attention appears to be elsewhere; and the man reciprocates by stroking her breasts. This is the 'piercing' embrace. (22b-24a).

During a fair, or on a long pilgrimage, or in total darkness, or in a secluded place if the bodies of a man and a woman happen to touch for a short while, this is known as the 'rubbing' embrace by the great sage Vatsyayana. (24b-26a).

When, under circumstances similar to the ones above, if the man and woman happen to get squeezed against a wall then the embrace is called the 'squeezing'. (26b-27a).

In the last two embraces the couple may not even know each other, but lust incites them. (27b).

KISSING (CUMBANA)

The special play of the teeth, lips and tongue between inflamed loving couples is known as kissing. (28).

Kissing ranges from a mere peck on the cheeks to deep and erotic mouth to mouth contact. Kissing parts of the body can also give erotic pleasure.

There are fourteen types of kisses: special (nimitta), sucking (sphurita), thrusting (ghattita), equal (sama), oblique (tiryak), churning (bhranta), pressing (avapidita), catching the teeth (dvijagraha), covering (samputaka), tongue-war (jihva-yuddha), two forms of awakening (prabodhita), shadow (chaya) and transferred (samkranta). (29-30).

Forehead, eyes, cheeks, lips, tongue, neck and chest are the usual places for kissing. Sometimes forehead, navel, pubic region and armpits are also kissed. According to the learned the parts of the body that can be kissed depend on local custom and usage. (32-33a).

When a man forces his lips onto her lips but she pretends to be unconcerned, this is the 'special' kiss. (33b-34).

When a woman attempts to thirstily suck the lips of her beloved with her mouth it is the 'sucking' kiss. (35).

She covers his eyes with her hands and thrusts her tongue into his mouth. This is known as the 'thrusting' kiss. The three kinds of kisses described above are specially suitable for the newly married. (36-37).

When both the lips come into full contact, it is called the 'equal' kiss. (38a).

In the kiss known as 'oblique' the man takes, from the side, the entire leaf-like lips of his beloved into his rounded mouth. (38b-39a).

When the lover, who is standing behind her, seizes her curly tresses, turns her head around and kisses her round lotus lips this is the 'charming' kiss. (39b-40).

If the equal, oblique and charming kisses are done

roughly they become the 'pressing' kiss. (41).

When the lover pulls her lower lip out a little with the thumb and index finger and kisses her teeth with his lips, this is known as the 'catching the teeth' kiss. (42).

If a woman or a clean shaven man holds and gently presses the lips of the other partner with his/her lips this, according to Vatsyayana, is the 'covering' kiss. (43-44a).

The covering kiss becomes the 'tongue-war' kiss if the partners playfully duel with their tongues. (44b).

When the woman is fast asleep and the man comes in and awakens her with a kiss, this is known as the 'awakening' kiss. (45).

At times the woman pretends to be asleep when the man covers her eyes and kisses her. This is the 'beloved's' kiss, a variety of the 'awakening' kiss. (46).

When two lovers kiss each other's portraits or mirror reflections it is known as the 'shadow' kiss. This is done either to show passionate desire or to make up after a love quarrel. (47).

Kissing a statue, or a child or a picture to convey love is the 'transferred' kiss. (48).

NAIL MARKS (NAKHA-KSATA)

Little scars made on the body by lovers are known as nail marks. There are nine types of marks. They are known as: clashing (churitaka), crescent (ardha-candra), circle (mandalaka), line (rekha), tiger-claw (vyaghra-pada), peacock's footprint (mayura-padaka), hare leap (sasa-pluta), lotus petal (utpalaka) and mementos (smaraka). Armpits, arms, thighs, flanks, back, chest, neck and breasts are marked with nails when lovers are in the grip of tremendous passion. (49-52).

Pain and sexual pleasure have always been related and are inherited by us from our animal ancestry. People who get sexually worked up by causing pain are known as sadists and those who find sexual excitement in receiving pain are called masochists. Though exclusive and intense sadism and masochism are both physically harmful and undesirable, a little harmless expression of pain may add to heightened sexual arousal. Love bites, scratching with nails and love blows are examples of mild and harmless sadism and masochism. Indian erotic texts, with their love for elaborate classifications have codified many types of bites, nail marks and love blows.

Love making with nails is commonly done just after a love quarrel, at first love making, in the midst of coitus, during foreplay, on the day of the spring festival, before going on a long journey, on reaching puberty and, for those in the grip of sexual desire, anytime. (53-54a).

When a lover touches the breasts, neck, cheeks, thighs and pubic region of his beloved with the nails of the left hand, her hair stands on end. If at this moment, light marks are made with a clicking of nails they are called the 'clashing'. (54b-56a).

Small semi-circular marks made on the neck and breasts are called the 'crescent'. When two crescents are made facing each other they become the 'circle'. (56b-57a).

A mark two finger-breadths long on the neck, thigh or the entrance of the love house is called the 'line'. A crooked line becomes the 'tiger-claw'. (57b-58).

If all the nails are brought together to mark the nipples it is known as the 'peacock's footprint' by the scholars. (59).

Curved marks placed together around the nipples are examples of the 'hare-leap'. (60).

Petal-like nail marks on the breasts, buttocks and hips are called 'lotus petals' by the wise. (61).

Three or four lines made on the beloved's breasts, arms and lips as a keepsake before going on a long journey are known as 'mementos' by the writers of erotica. (62-63a).

TEETH MARKS (DANTA-KSATA)

Biting erogenous zones of each other's body by passionate young couples is called teeth marks. (63b).

Teeth marks are of eight kinds: hidden (gudhaka), swollen (ucchunaka), dot (bindu), coral beads (pravala manita), necklace of dots (bindumala), pearl necklace (manimala), broken clouds (khanda-abhraka) and boar bite (kroda-carvita). (64-65).

With the exception of the inside of the mouth, upper lip and eyes, teeth marks can be made on all other parts of the body that are fit for kissing. (66)

A bite made on the lower lip in the grip of passion is called the 'hidden'. Biting the lower lip or the cheeks with a little pressure so that it swells up is the 'swollen' bite. (67-68a).

A small bite made in the middle of the lower lip with just two teeth is known as the 'dot' by Vatsyayana. (68b-69a).

Those that know the scriptures of love say that if, after a lot of practice, the teeth and lips are brought together to leave a symbolic row of red marks on the lower lip it is the 'coral beads' mark. (69b-70)

A row of dot-like marks made with only two teeth on the thighs or forehead are called the 'necklace of dots'. (71).

The necklace of dots becomes the 'necklace of pearls' if the marks are made with all the sharp teeth. (72).

Irregular and circular marks, either large, small or minute, made simultaneously with all the teeth, in the armpits, on the forehead, on the neck, on the breasts and in the groins are known as the 'broken clouds'. (73-74).

A red, long and unbroken line of teeth marks is an example of the 'boar bite'. (75).

Thus ends the third chapter on outer love play between the hero and his heroine in the work called 'Rati-ratna-pradipika' by King Devaraja Maharaja, the Elder.

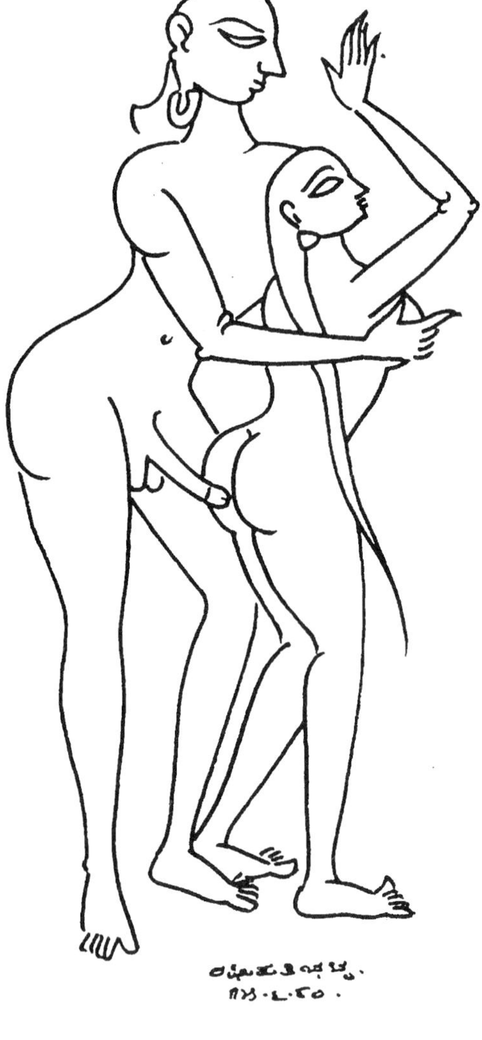

Vicitra

INNER LOVE (ABHYANTARA-RATI)

The coming together of the penis and the vagina is called inner love. There are twenty-seven ways of performing the sex act. (1).

Human beings are perhaps the only animals on earth that have sex face to face. But this is not the only way to make love. Human anatomy allows considerable mobility and dexterity. We can turn and twist our bodies in many ways and it would not be a bad idea if we tried to have sexual intercourse in other and more experimental positions. Though the large number of sexual postures described in traditional Indian texts on erotics may not be easy to perform for most people with delicate or heavy bodies, their value lies in suggesting both variety and experimentation in the sexual act. They point to a new direction in love making, and who knows, many young and athletic lovers may benefit from their variety.

These twenty-seven ways can be sub-divided into three groups of nine each based on the size of the genitals (pramana), time taken to reach orgasm (kala) and the force of desire (bhava).

The three unions, between gazelle woman and hare man, mare woman and bull man and elephant woman and horse man, are the 'equal' (sama) unions. When gazelle and bull and mare and horse unite these are 'high' (ucca) unions. Coming together of elephant with bull and mare with hare are called 'lower' (nica) unions. Sexual intercourse between gazelle and horse is 'very high' (ati-ucca) and between elephant and hare

is 'very low' (ati-nica). These nine are based on the size of genitals. Now the division based on the time taken to reach orgasm. (2-6).

Men can be divided into three groups based on the time they take to ejaculate: quick (laghu-drava), medium (madhya-drava) and long (cira-drava). Similarly, women can also be divided into three groups, on the basis of the time they take to reach orgasm. (7).

Sexual intercourse is a physical act in which the penis is inserted into the vagina and moved in and out repeatedly. This movement is usually slow in the beginning but becomes more and more rapid and violent as arousal and pleasure increase. To help penetration and the pumping movement the vulvovaginal glands secrete lubricating fluids. The continual in and out movement of the penis within the vagina exerts repeated pressure against the clitoris and the sensitive labia giving pleasurable sensations to the woman. Similarly, the friction of the sensitive tip of the penis, including the delicate prepuce area, contributes to male excitement and pleasure. In popular myth and imagination, it is believed that a large penis deep in the vagina gives the woman sexual delight. This is not at all physiologically true. The vagina is poorly supplied with nerve endings and is relatively insensitive. The pleasure that a woman feels at having a penis inside her is purely psychological. The real sexual stimulation is provided by the outer organs of the clitoris and the vaginal lips. It is unlikely that any woman could actually distinguish between a four inch and seven inch penis once it is inside her.

The concern and interest in penis size and the myth that a large penis can give more satisfaction is a total fallacy based on cultural or visual considerations.

After a period of thrusting and back and forth movement by both partners a peak of sexual excitement is reached which is called the orgasm. In the man, the semen flows into the urethral tube running through the penis making it swell to three times its normal size. Then, a series of muscular spasms shoot the semen out into the vagina. The spasms and contractions that accompany the ejaculation of semen produce the delightful and ecstatic joy of orgasm.

As the woman reaches orgasm she too experiences muscular spasms that involve most of the muscles of the body, including those in the external sexual organs. Contractions of the muscles around the entrance of the vagina press against the end of the penis to increase sexual pleasure at the time of orgasm.

There are a complicated set of muscles around the vagina and anus. During orgasm some of these contract automatically, while others can be contracted by conscious attempt. If women learn to voluntarily contract these muscles they can press and grip the end of the penis tightly to produce added enjoyment for both partners.

Orgasm does not always mean satisfaction and there is a lot of difference in response between the two sexes. After the male orgasm the penis becomes flaccid and at least about thirty minutes or more are required before another erection. A woman, however, can be satisfied either by one orgasm or many desire repeated orgasms at very short intervals.

According to modern research sexual activity, from arousal to orgasm, can be divided into three distinct phases. The first is called the Excitement phase which involves foreplay and early intercourse. The second Plateau phase occurs when intercourse is well advanced and both the partners are in the midst of intense excitement. The last is the Orgasmic phase when both the partners are in a state of physical tension. In this phase there is muscular tension, high pulse rate, quick breathing and elevated blood pressure. After orgasm there is a period of recovery which varies in the two sexes, as already mentioned. The time between the first (Excitement) and last (Orgasmic) phases also varies from person to person and can be anything from a few minutes to half an hour or more (see Ward, 1984 and Trimmer, 1978).

Couples who reach orgasm at the same time are called 'equal' (sama). The unions of a quick woman with a moderate man and a moderate woman with a long man are known as 'high' (ucca). The two 'low' (nica) unions are between a moderate woman and a quick man and a long woman with a quick man. When a quick woman and a long man, or a long woman and a quick man unite these become the extremes of 'very high' (ati-ucca) and 'very low' (ati-nica) respectively. (8-11a).

Women and men can be further divided into three groups each according to the force of their sexual desire (bhava or vega): mild (manda), moderate (madhya) and furious (canda). Among these, 'equal' unions are between those whose libido is similar. Mild woman with a moderate man and a moderate woman with a furious man are 'high' unions. 'Low' unions are between a moderate woman and a mild man and a furious woman with a moderate man. Intercourse between a mild woman and a furious man and a furious woman with a mild man are examples of 'very high' and 'very low' unions respectively. There are nine groups in each division based on genital size (pramana), time to reach orgasm (kala) and force of desire (bhava or vega). (11b-15).

Coitus based on genital size (pramana):

Gazelle (harini) + hare (sasa)

mare (vadava) + bull (vrsa) = Equal (sama)

elephant (hastini) + horse (asva)

gazelle + bull/mare + horse = High (ucca)

elephant + bull/mare + hare = Low (nica)

gazelle + horse = Very high (ati-ucca)

elephant + hare = Very low (ati-nica)

Coitus based on orgasm time (kala):

quick (laghu) + quick (laghu)

moderate (madhya) + moderate (madhya) = Equal

long (cira) + long (cira) (sama)

quick + moderate & moderate + long = High (ucca)

moderate + quick & long + moderate = Low (nica)

quick + long = Very high (ati-ucca)

long + quick = Very low (ati-nica)

Coitus based on force of desire (vega or bhava):

mild (manda) + mild (manda)

moderate (madhya) + moderate (madhya) = Equal

furious (canda) + furious (canda) (sama)

mild + moderate & moderate + furious = High (ucca)

moderate + mild & furious + moderate = Low (nica)

mild + furious = Very high (ati-ucca)

furious + mild = Very low (ati-nica)

According to the opinion of the scholar Kokkoka, equal combinations are the best. The two varieties of high and low unions are moderately good. The extremes of very high and very low are improper. (16-17a).

The reference to Kokkoka is from *Rati-rahasya,* Chapter III, verses 5-10.

Women do not feel sexually aroused or fulfilled in the low form of intercourse, because there is not enough friction between the inner vagina and the penis. In the high unions there is pain and discomfort within the delicate inner lips of the vagina and so the woman remains dry and dissatisfied. Mutual gratification is everything in sex as the god of love rules the mind. (17b-19a).

There are small blood born animalcules in the woman's vagina that produce mild, moderate or very intense irritation. This irritable itch can be diminished only by the vigorous friction of the male flagpole (penis) that stimulates the flow of love juices. Initially, however, the flow is uncomfortable and unpleasant. But at the end of intercourse she reaches blissful

orgasm similar to the male ejaculation. One moment she screams, at another she cries and dances with joy. Unable to bear the ecstasy she closes her eyes in delirium. For lovers sexual gratification is the greatest tranquillity. That is why, along with the Great Sage, I prescribe the following remedy for true enlightenment: union with a thousand vaginas. (19b-24).

There is a clear pun on the word 'Bhaga'. Derived from the Sanskrit root √ bhaj (sevayam : bhvadi-gana) = to serve, to possess, to enjoy: it has a wide variety of meanings: the Sun god, the moon, a form of Lord Siva, happiness, affluence, fame, beauty, excellence, love, pleasure, virtue, final beatitude, omnipotence, power, desire, knowledge and the vagina.

In this there is probably a reference to an ancient alchemical (rasayana-sastra) belief shared by both Indian Tantra and Chinese Taoism.

Tantra and Tao principles hold that the universe is composed of two forces: active and passive, Sakti and Siva, female and male or yang (male-active) and yin (female-passive). It was believed that if these two opposing forces could be harmonized within the body, human beings could become immortal. But old age and loss of semen during sexual intercourse are two very common ways in which the yang or male essence of strength, power and long life can be lost. When yang starts declining in the human body it needs to be replenished with yin shui, the water of yin or vaginal secretions. Therefore when a man is engaged in coitus he should not ejaculate his semen. Not only should he retain his semen but learn to absorb the female secretions from his partner which contain yin shui. The more yin shui he absorbs the more male essence is strengthened. Frequent sexual intercourse is therefore essential for long life. Many Tantrik and Taoist techniques teach how to have multiple sexual intercourse and suck the sexual fluids back into the body. In China, the famous Yellow Emperor Huang Ti (2697 B.C.) slept with more than one thousand women to suck away their sexual energy and become immortal. In more recent times, Mao Zedong, the great

Communist Emperor, attempted to sleep with numerous young virgins to preserve his youth (Li, 1996). Though he, and all others who have tried this misguided technique have failed to achieve everlasting life, the reference to a thousand 'bhagas' here may imply such Taoist and Tantrik left-handed (vamacara) sexual practices.

The Yellow Emperor Huang Ti is also credited with the compilation of the first sex manual. This unusual early classic describes techniques for kissing, titillating the erogenous zones and timing of pelvic thrusts during intercourse. The work is in the form of a dialogue between the Emperor and three women.

According to the Commentator 'thousand Bhagas' is when the couple climaxes together. And simultaneous sexual climax is only possible in an equal union. (25-26a).

If the word 'Muni' (Great Sage) refers to Vatsyayana then the word 'Bhasyakrt' (Commentator) stands for Yasodhara, the 13th century author of *Jayamangala*, the most exhaustive and complete commentary on the *Kama-sutra*. Kancinatha, the commentator on the 13th century erotic work *Rati-rahasya* by Kokkoka, also identifies Muni with Vatsyayana.

The lover should receive his beloved in a house decorated with bright lamps, flower garlands, fragrance of incense and filled with friends and associates. He should then seat her on his left side and entertain her with amusing and metaphorical tales. Gradually, embracing her with his left arm, he should touch her breasts through the Kancipura silk covering. He can then arouse her sexual desire with erotic stories and bawdy love songs and surreptitiously dispatch the assembly. He may now kiss her chin and cheeks making the 'sit' sound with his tongue and palate. He can now make the 'churita' nail mark below her navel, on her breasts, thighs and waist. He can also loosen her girdle. If she resists he should kiss her cheeks and rub her love house with the top of his penis. He ought to then hold her mouth against his own and tightly squeeze her

between his arms, gently stroking her love house with his hands. (26b-32).

The texture of the inner vagina can be of four kinds: soft like the lotus bud, uneven like the skin on the fingers, wrinkled and rough like a cow's tongue. Each is softer and more desirable than the next. (33-34).

At the front of the vulva is a small penis like bud—swing of the love god—which is extremely sensitive to touch. When stimulated with the fingers, this Cupid's parasol lubricates the vaginal region with a flow of love fluid.

Just at the entrance of the woman's house of love is a nose shaped organ called the Cupid's parasol. This is filled with vessels that secrete love juices. Not very far from the opening of the love house is a full-moon shaped gland that also fills with sexual fluids. There are many other female sexual organs but these three are the most important, particularly for finger stimulation. (35-39).

The Cupid's parasol (Kama-atapatra) probably refers to the clitoris and the full-moon shaped gland (purna-candra-abhidha-nadi) to the larger lips (labia majora) of the vagina. These lips are folds of skin around the vaginal opening with underlying deposits of fat. Anatomically, they are considered to be the female counterpart of the male scrotum. Their outer parts are covered with hair but their inner surface is smooth and moist from the secretions of the various glands. Also, sweat glands on the labia majora secrete a sexual odour.

Snake's hood (phanindra bhoga), half moon (ardha candra), elephant's trunk (kari hasta) and Cupid's goad (smara ankusa) are some of the methods of vaginal stimulation using the index and middle fingers.

The lover should bring his beloved to sexual readiness by exciting her love house with nail marks, bites and finger play. He can then proceed to the various love postures. (40-41).

There are five major sexual postures: supine (uttana), lateral (tiryak), sitting (asita), standing (sthita) and bending

Vestita

(anata). Now the many variations of these basic five. (42).

A long list of sexual positions: (1) rustic (gramya), (2) urban (nagarika), (3) blossoming (utphulla), (4) gaping (jrmbhita), (5) Indra's wife (Indrani), (6) basket (samputa), (7) back-basket (parsva-samputa), (8) squeezing (pidita), (9) clasping (vestita), (10) mare's (vadava), (11) bent upwards (udbhugnaka), (12) half-body squeeze (ardha-anga-pidita), (13) yawning (jrmbha), (14) spread out (prasarita), (15) bamboo splitting (venu vidarita), (16) spear point (sulanka), (17) crab like (karkati), (18) swinging (prenkhaka), (19) lotus seat (padmasana), (20) half lotus seat (ardha padmasana), (21) snake's noose (phani pasa), (22) revolving (paravrtta), (23) controlled (samyama), (24) tortoise like (kaurma), (25) casket (samudgaka), (26) turning away (parivartita), (27) two feet (yugma pada), (28) rubbing (vimardita), (29) monkey like (markata), (30) supported (asrita), (31) face-to-face (sammukha), (32) winner of three worlds (traivikramika), (33) two soles (dvitalaka), (34) knee-elbow (janu kurpara), (35) hanging (avalambita), (36) cow like (dhenuka), (37) elephant like (aibhika), (38) multiple group (samghata), (39) herd of cows (goyutha), (40) water sport (vari kelita), (41) man like (paurusa), (42) humming bee like (bhramara), (43) oscillating (prenkholitaka), (44) massaging (mardana), (45) intoxicated (kohala), (46) rubbing from all sides (amardana), (47) vulva pressing (yoni pidana), (48) forced (nirghata), (49) boar thrust (varaha ghata), (50) bull thrust (vrsa ghata), (51) sparrow's play (cataka ullasita), and (52) tired-basket (sranta samputa). (43-50).

The woman lies on her back, with her hips behind the arms and thighs of her seated lover. This is called the rustic (gramya) position. (51)

If the woman's thighs rest between those of her lover, this becomes the urban (nagarika) posture. Those who know the art of sex say that these two postures are suitable for an equally matched couple. (52).

The woman props herself up on her hands and feet to bring her vulva closer to his penis. He in turn brings his thighs nearer and enjoys her while squeezing her breasts. This is the blossoming (utphullaka) method. (53).

The woman lies on her bed. She turns and raises herself a little to open her thighs and expose her vulva. This is the gaping (jrmbhita) position. (54).

The woman rests on her bed, raises her soft thighs and holds the lover's sides between her knees. This is known as Indra's wife (Indranika). According to the learned this formation can be performed only after a lot of practice. (55).

Thus ends the fourth chapter on inner love in the work called 'Rati-ratna-pradipika' by King Devaraja the Elder.

Asvasamyoga

POSTURES OF INNER SEX PLAY (ABHYANTARA-RATAU KARANA-NIRUPANA)

If the couple engage in coitus with their thighs spread straight out together this is the basket (samputa) pose. (1).

If the couple in the basket posture turn to their side it becomes the back-basket (parsva-samputa). If in the back-basket they press their thighs together the posture is called squeezing (pidita). The squeezing becomes clasping (vestita) if the thighs are crossed. If in the basket pose the woman sucks the young lover's penis in and out with the force of the lips of her vagina it is known as the mare's (vadava) posture. (2-3).

Samputa Vadava

Around the opening of the vagina is a network of muscles. Of these, two sets are important: the constrictor cunni which opens and closes the vaginal entrance, and the levator muscles that contract and relax the vaginal passage. A woman can learn to consciously control these muscles with special exercises. Such conscious control can be of help in childbirth, to strengthen orgasm and increase male pleasure by firmly pressing and gripping the penis at the time of ejaculation.

The woman, who is lying on a bed with her thighs outstretched, is lifted up a little and embraced. She in turn places her feet on her lover's chest. They then sexually please each other. This is the bent upwards (udbhugnaka) posture. (4).

While in the bent upwards pose, if the doe-eyed woman lifts one leg up the position becomes the half-body squeeze (ardha-anga-pidita). (5)

In the yawning (jrmbhaka) form of intercourse the woman lifts her thighs and places her feet on her lover's shoulders. (6).

The yawning posture is transformed into the spread out (prasarita) pose if the woman, who is reclining on a bed, extends one leg sideways for her lover to enjoy her. (7).

If in the yawning attitude the woman continually alternates her feet from one side to the other it becomes the bamboo splitting (venu vidarita) position. (8).

A woman who is resting with her hips raised up lifts one leg so that the foot touches her head and bends the other leg sideways this is known as the spear point (sulanka) posture. (9).

The woman bends her lifted legs so that the soles of her feet touch each other. The man presses his navel region against her, lifts her waist a little, and squats to enjoy her. This pose is known as crab like (kauliraka or karkati) and is considered to be very mature and enjoyable during intercourse. (10).

If, while in the crab-like position, the woman gently rocks her beloved from side to side, then the pose is known as the

Jrmbhaka

Venuvidarita

Kauliraka or Karkati

Padmasana

swinging (prenkhaka). (11).

She places her left foot on her right thigh and the right foot on her left thigh. She then holds her lover up and plays with him. This is the lotus (padmasana) form. (12).

If in the lotus posture only one leg is crossed then it is transformed into the half lotus seat (ardha padmasana) position. (13).

While lying on her back the woman passes her arms from under her thighs and embraces her lover's neck waiting for him to penetrate. He holds her neck by passing his arms from under her knees and unites with her; this is the snake's noose (phani pasa) pose. (14).

In the revolving (paravrtta) posture the man lies with his back turned away from his beloved. The woman embraces him and turns him around to make love. (15).

Samyama

Samudgaka

Parivartita

Yugmapada

Asrita

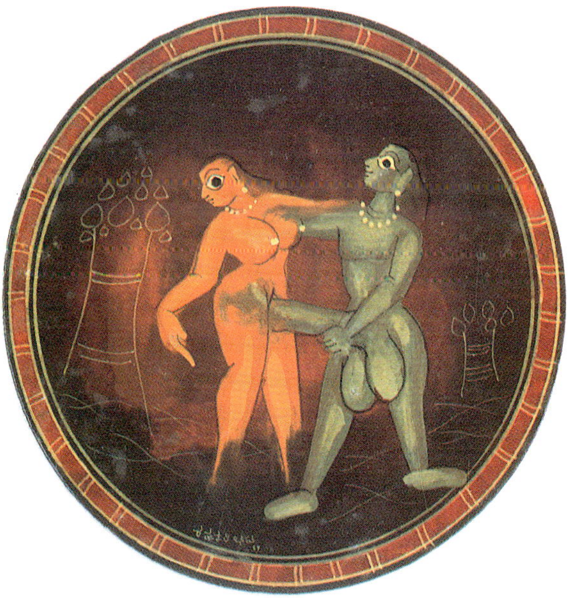

The woman, who is resting on a bed, raises herself to hold her toes with her fingers. The supine lover passes his arms from under her knees and embraces her neck to unite with her. This union, according to sexually experienced scholars such as Mallanaga, is called the controlled (samyama). (16).

Mallanaga, author of the *Kama-sutra*. Vatsyayana was his family name.

With their arms and legs stretched out, they lie one on top of the other. He makes love to her in this tortoise (kaurma) position by placing his mouth to her mouth, his thighs on her thighs and his arms on her arms. (17).

From bent upwards to tortoise are ordinary (sadharana) supine (uttana) postures. Now we come to the lateral (tiryag) poses: a woman lies with her body in a curve. The man puts his thighs between her thighs, embraces her and has sex with her. This is called the casket (samudgaka). (19).

While in the casket position if either the man or the woman turns around it becomes the turning away (parivartita). (20).

The seated woman bends her feet and puts them together. The lover lifts her up and unites with her laterally, this is the two feet (yugma pada) union. (21).

He sits between his beloved's knees; then turns his hips a little and copulates with her in the sitting position. This is known as the rubbing (vimarditaka). (22).

If during the rubbing manner the lovers face each other it is called the monkey-like posture (markatam).

Now the standing forms: (23).

If the lover rests his beloved's back against a wall or a pillar, embraces her and unites with her from the front this is called the supported (asrita) congress. (24).

While still in the supported union if the lover lifts one of his beloved's legs and rests it on his elbow this is the face-to-face (sammukha). (25).

Sammukha

Trivikrama

The woman is still in the supported position, and the man bends her leg upwards and embraces her, this is known as the winner of the three worlds (traivikrama). (26).

He leans against a wall for support and places his hands at the level of the navel. She puts the soles of her feet on top of his hands and lowers herself a little. Sitting comfortably in this manner she holds and embraces his neck and unites with him. This is the two soles (dvitalaka) union. (27).

In the knee-elbow (janu kurpara) congress, the man stands holding the woman's knee and neck between his elbows. She holds on to his waist and unites with him. (28).

She sits in the palm of his hands, embraces his neck with her forearms and entwines her thighs around his waist while he stands resting against a wall. She strikes her feet against the wall, makes 'sit' sounds and takes deep gasping breaths while they make love. This is the hanging (avalambita) pose. (29).

She rests her hands and feet on the ground and he enters her like a bull would. This is the cow-like (dhenuka) position. (30).

Dhenuka

Aibhika

Varahagata

Samghata

She places her breasts, head and face on the ground and raises her rear. He titillates her vulva with his fingers before uniting with her. This is the elephant-like (aibhika) congress. (31).

Antelopes, donkeys, young horses, buffaloes and goats: these are some of the four-legged animals whose congress can be imitated by a clever man. (32).

Picturesque postures (vicitram)

Two women who trust each other lie with their heads in opposite directions but with their loins crossing. The lover sits near them and excites their love line with forms of outer love play. When the passion of one of them is aroused he makes love to her. This is called multiple (samghata) congress. (33).

Under the influence of tremendous passion, the man and the two women lying with their thighs crossed, may make love to each other. (34).

If in a group of friendly women a young man makes love to each woman in turn this is called the herd of cows (goyutha).

When a single woman unites with many men one after another, this is also known as the herd of cows. (35).

Water sport (vari kelita) coitus is when a man makes love to many women like one bull elephant that mounts many cow elephants while they sport in a lake. (36).

In the famous kingdom of women (stri-rajya) one woman has sex with many men. On the other hand, in Karnataka, one man enjoys sex with many women. (37).

Either with her lover's permission or just to please her own desire, if a woman mounts her supine lover this is known as the man-like (paurusa or purusayita) congress. (38).

When a woman who has mounted her lover in the male fashion places her lover's penis into her vagina and rocks her hips from side to side this is the humming bee-like (bhramara) variety of the man-like union. (39).

When a woman, who is on top of her supine lover, holds on to some support and jumps up and down this is the oscillating (prenkholita) union. (40).

Purusayita

Women who are in an advanced stage of pregnancy, who have just delivered a baby, who are fat and heavy, who are very thin and belong to the gazelle class, who are menstruating, or who have not yet reached puberty should not try the man-like positions. (41).

A man may hold the root of his erect penis and insert it into the love house of his beloved who rests with her thighs spread apart. If he then stirs his penis inside her this is known as the massaging (mardana) by scholars. (42).

A man who has just inserted the top of his penis suddenly bends his hips and thrusts his penis into her vagina, this is known as the intoxicated (kohala). The opposite of this (when he only moves his penis about near the vulva) is called rubbing from all sides (amardana or avamardana). (43).

When a man presses his penis very hard and for a long time on the vulva so that it hurts, this is the vulva pressing (yoni pidana). (44).

Mardana

Kohala

Yonipidana

Cataka Ullasita

Srantasamputa

Srantasamputa

In the forced (nirghata) coitus, the man repeatedly and quickly moves his penis in and out of the vagina. (45).

In the mode known as the boar thrust (varaha ghata) by scholars, the man thrusts his penis into any one side of the vagina. (46).

If a man alternately thrusts his penis against each side of the vagina this becomes the bull thrust (vrsa ghata). (47).

If a man who has inserted his penis into the vagina shakes it inside three or four times this is the sparrow's play (cataka ullasita). (48).

After a hectic session of love play the man places his lips on the lips of his doe-eyed beloved, his chest against her breasts and his penis inside her vagina and rests like this for a long while this is the tired basket (sranta samputa). (49).

Thus ends the fifth chapter on postures of inner sex play in the work called 'Rati-ratna-pradipika' by King Devaraja the Elder.

Mardana

6TH CHAPTER

SUPERIOR COITUS OR 'ORAL' SEX (AUPARISTAKA)

Now we shall look at the special love-relationships (sanjna) that result from sexual unions. There are eight such love-relationships. (1).

The first love-relationship is called passionate love (ragavat), the second is incidental love (aharyaraga). The next is artificial love (krtrima), after which comes substitute love (vyavahita). Then there is love with an eunuch (pota-sanjna) and love by deceit (khala). There is free love (ayantrika) and also love after a quarrel (pranayadikali). (2-3).

Love starts from the day they see each other. The young couple's love at first sight grows. Efforts are made to bring them together with the help of go-betweens. Finally their efforts are rewarded and the lovers meet and make love. This first sexual union is an example of passionate (ragavat) love. Passionate love can happen when two people come together after long separation. The knowers of sexology say that when lovers who have quarrelled make up and have sexual intercourse this is also a form of passionate love. (4-6).

If two people unite in sex either for monetary gain or to overcome some trouble this is known as incidental love (aharyaraga). Love between mediators is also incidental love. (7-8a).

If a man who loves another woman, or a woman who loves another man has sex with a third person this is called artificial (krtrima) love. (8b-9a).

Ragavat

Ragavat

Krtrima

If a man who has his real beloved in mind even before starting intercourse... [but has sex with another woman thinking of his real beloved, this is substitute love (vyavahita)]. (9b).

The description of substitute love (vyavahita raga) is incomplete. One line between verses 9b and 10a is missing from both the editions consulted. A footnote on page 39 of the Mysore edition says: *vyavahitasya laksanamatra na drsyate* = the definition of vyavahita is not seen here. This not entirely correct. Only half the definition is missing. I have completed it on the basis of *Kama-sutra* (II, 10, 21).

Sexually excited by erotic thoughts a man makes love to an eunuch who superficially resembles a woman. This is love with an eunuch (pota sanjna). (10).

Khala

The rape of an elderly, defenceless prostitute by an uncouth half-wit is love by deceit (khala). (11).

When a charming trickster manages to befriend a trusting village girl for a long period of unrestrained sexual fun, this is free love (aniyantrita). (12-13a).

In the middle of passionate sexual intercourse the woman begins to talk about her co-wives. Imagining her beloved's unfaithful conduct she starts to cry. She works herself into a frenzy, seizes and pulls her lover's hair, beats herself and uses coarse speech. She turns away from him in anger and drops the bed clothes on the floor. She discards her ornaments and sits weeping on the doorstep. Seeing her throwing a fit the lover should use all means of reconciliation to pacify her. He should promise to give her gifts and divert her attention. When she is reconciled and happy again the lover lays her down on the bed and unites with her. This is the love after a quarrel (panayakali or pranayakalaha). (13b-18).

Alternately, (in another variation of the same love) to gain her favour the lover attempts to use gentle words to change her mood and promises to give her presents and ornaments. He even falls at her feet. If however all this fails he suddenly turns violent and treats her with disrespect. (19-20).

Superior coitus or oral sex

The sexual act that takes place between the thighs and the mouth is called superior coitus (auparistaka). (21).

I have used the expression 'superior coitus' to translate 'auparistaka' after Alan Danielou (1994: 183) as this appears to be the most appropriate rendering of the Sanskrit term.

Oral sex involves the use of lips, tongue and mouth in a sexual way. It is a very intimate form of relationship as a woman takes a man's penis into her mouth and stimulates it by licking, sucking and kissing. This act is known as fellatio. This technique can be used merely as a form of foreplay or may lead to orgasm, replacing vaginal intercourse. Kissing and licking the glans penis or the testicles is technically called 'penilingus'. When the penis is inserted into the mouth and the man makes in and out thrusting movement while the woman's mouth remains still is known as 'irrumatio'.

Oral stimulation of the female genitals is known as cunnilingus and includes kissing and licking the vulva and inserting the tongue into the vagina. Though the woman's mouth is not as deep as the vagina many prefer oral sex because of the greater muscular strength and control of the mouth and the tremendous dexterity of the tongue. Similarly, even though the man's tongue is much shorter than the penis, many women enjoy cunnilingus more that genital penetration as the tongue has greater mobility and versatility. When oral sex is performed simultaneously by both partners with their bodies facing opposite directions this is the famous 'soixante-neuf' or '69' in common slang.

Oral sex however demands a very high standard of hygiene and immaculate cleanliness. Also, in these days of AIDS it is better to restrict oral sex to known partners, or use condoms (see Ward, 1984 and Trimmer, 1978).

This can take two forms: the one performed by women (fellatio) and that which is done by men (cunnilingus).

There are eight methods of oral sex for women. These are: (1) regular (nimitta), (2) side-biting (parsva damsa), (3) external bite (bahisamdamsa), (4) internal bite (antassamdamsa), (5) kissing and stroking (cumbita-parimrstaka), (6) mango sucking (amracusita)...and (8) devouring (sangara). (22-24a).

The woman holds her lover's penis in her hand and brings her lips close to it. Then, suddenly, saying that she cannot do it, shakes the glans and angrily releases it. This is the regular (nimitta) manner. (24b-26a).

She covers the head of the penis with her hands and bites the sides gently without using her teeth. 'Enough!' she utters, again and again. This is the side-biting (parsva damsa) variety. (26b-27).

Parsvadamsa

Bahisamdamsa

After repeated requests from her lover, she puts his penis in her mouth and presses it by tightening her lips around it. She sucks the glans and makes 'vasat' and 'sit' sounds. As she bites the foreskin, this is known as the external bite (bahisamdamsa). (28-29).

"That is enough now" she says. But after frequent appeals from the lover she presses the penis and takes the glans into her mouth. She then stimulates it with her lips until the man ejaculates. This is called internal bite (antassamdamsa) because she bites the glans penis inside her mouth. (30-31).

Covering his Cupid's instrument with her hand she kisses only the glans as if she is kissing his lips. This is the kissing (cumbita) variety. (32).

Kissing the top of the penis, she covers it with her tongue to block the flow of ejaculation, this is the stroking (parimrstaka) variety. (33).

Cumbita

The woman puts half of the erect penis in her mouth, presses on it and then repeatedly sucks it in hard like when sucking a mango fruit. This is called mango sucking (amra cusita). (34-35a).

She takes the entire erect penis into her mouth and stimulates it with her tongue and lips until he ejaculates. She then kisses the penis making 'vasat' sounds. This is the well known devouring (sangara) oral technique. (35b-37a).

Vatsyayana says that all women do not perform fellatio. Only unchaste and wanton women, prostitutes and servant and attendant girls do it. Women of good family usually avoid oral sex. (37b-38).

Men also do oral sex with women in eight different ways. These are: (1) lip-trembling (adhara sphurita), (2) tongue-roving (jihvabhramanaka), (3) tongue-stroking (jihvamardita), (4) sucking (cusita), (5) sucking-dry (ucchusaka), (6) agitating (ksobhaka), (7) much-sucking (bahucusita) and (8) the love jewel (kakiladirata). (39-41a).

He gently sucks and kisses the two decorative lips of the vagina. This is the lip-trembling (adhara sphurita) method. (41b-42a).

He parts the outer lips of the vagina with his nose and thrusts his tongue into it and then moves it around. This is the tongue-roving (jihvabhramanaka). (42b-43a).

At first the lover stimulates the vulva with his nose, lips and chin. Then, pressing and pulling apart the lips of the vagina with his tongue he jams it into the battlefield of the love god. He then massages the inside again and again. This is the famous tongue-stroking (jihvamardita) technique. (43b-45).

After using the tongue techniques if the lover sucks in the vaginal secretions with his lips this is the sucking (cusita) method. (46).

The young lover lifts the thighs of his beloved a little with his hands and licks the navel area with his tongue. He clasps the lips of the vagina and enters his tongue inside. He rotates his tongue around in the vagina until the love fluids flow. He then sucks them all dry. This is the sucking-dry (ucchusita) manner. (47-49a).

Parting her thighs and placing his head between them he agitates the vulva with his tongue. When she lubricates he drinks the fluid with his tongue. This is the agitating (ksobhaka). (49b-50).

Vicitra Goyutha

The woman is on a high pedestal and the man sits near her feet. He supports her waist with an embrace on his shoulders and strokes her love house with his nose. When her juices flow he sucks them in. This form of oral sex is called much-sucking (bahucusita). (51-53a).

Alternately, both the lovers rest on a bed and kiss and mutually excite each other's genitals. This is the love jewel (kakilarata) of oral coitus. These are all techniques of love making. (53b-54).

Now to consider the love blows (prahanana) that couples use during intercourse. There are ten varieties: (1) back-of-the-hand (apahasta), (2) hollow-of-the-palm (prasrtaka), (3) closed-fist (musti), (4) palm-and-fingers (samatala), (5) vertical-blow (kartari), (6) favourable-vertical-blow (bhadra-kartari), (7) double-vertical-blow (yama-kartari), (8) vertical-blow-with-sound (sabda-kartari), (9) stabbing-fist (viddha), and (10) pinching-the-flesh (samdamsaka). (55-57).

The sites on the body fit to receive love blows are the area between the breasts, on the head, both sides of the thighs, forehead and the pubic region. (58).

It seems rather odd that the author should have included just four verses on love blows in a chapter otherwise devoted to oral sex. Verses 55-58 should logically be in the seventh chapter which begins with a description of love blows. This is most certainly the scribe's mistake.

Thus ends the sixth chapter on superior coitus or 'oral' sex in the work called 'Rati-ratna-pradipika' by King Devaraja the Elder.

Goyutha

ALL MATTERS CONNECTED WITH SEX (SARVA-SURATA-ADHIKARA)

The young lover gently strikes his beloved's large breasts with the back of his hand throughout sexual intercourse. This is the back-of-the-hand-blow (apahasta). The lover can make 'him' sounds to heighten sexual pleasure. (1-2).

During coitus the young man bends his fingers and gently hits his beloved's head with the hollow of his hand making 'phut' sound. This is the hollow-of-the-palm (prasrtaka) love blow. 'Phut phut' and 'sit sit' are the proper sounds to make at this time. (3-4).

While the woman is either sitting on his knee or on a bed the man lovingly punches her with his fist. This is the closed-fist (musti) blow. At this the woman pretends to be offended and may roar, groan, cry and strike back. (5-6)

In the middle of sexual intercourse the lover extends his palm, spreads his fingers and plants a gentle blow on the cheeks and head. This is the palm-and-fingers (samatala). In response to this cruel violence she will cry like a goose, cuckoo or duck. (7-8).

When in sexual union from behind the lover strikes his beloved on the chest with the fist in which the index finger is extended this is called the vertical-blow (kartari). She makes erotic 'hin' sounds softly to herself. (9-10a).

In the favourable-vertical-blow (bhadra-kartari) the lover hits his beloved on the head with the index and middle fingers

Apahasta

extended out from his fist. 'Phut phut' sounds should be made by the woman. (10b-11).

If the man lovingly slaps his beloved on the head with both his hands in the vertical-blow mode it is known as the double-vertical-blow (yama-kartari). The woman should make 'phut' sounds. (12-13a).

During coitus, if the man plants a noisy vertical-blow on his woman's head, this is the vertical-blow-with-sound (sabda-kartari). Outwardly she makes the pretence of countering his blows, but secretly she makes very low erotic bird-like sounds. (13b-15a).

Gently slapping the cheeks of a woman with the index and middle fingers or middle and small fingers or with the thumb held away from the fist is called stabbing-fist (viddha). In response the woman starts crying uncontrollably. (15b-17a).

Pinching with the thumb and index fingers or the thumb and middle fingers is called biting-the-flesh (samdamsaka) because the action imitates actual biting. This is generally done on the breasts or the back and should be accompanied with 'sit' sounds. (17b-18).

The erotic sounds that are produced when love blows awaken passion are known as love cries (sitkrta) and defined by the ancient sage (Vatsyayana) as: (19)

The special sound that is produced from the throat to express pain caused by love blows is known as the 'sit-making' (sitkrtam). (20).

However, sit is not the only sound produced. There can be ten different love cries. They are: (1) 'hin' sound (hinkrta), (2) rumbling (stanita), (3) sighing (svasita), (4) crying (rudita), (5) moaning (kujita), (6) 'dhut' sound (dhutkrta), (7) 'phut' sound (phutkrta), (8) calling out for mother (ambartha), (9) words such as 'stop' or 'enough' (nisedhartha and alam-artha) and (10) words that ask for release or express pain (moksa-pidarthaka), cries of compassion (karunokti), rude and harsh words (snigdha-parusokti) and crow-like sounds (kakaruta). These are all examples of 'sit' making. (21-23).

That which seems to emanate from the ear and nasal region and vibrates in the head is called 'him' sound (himkrta). The sound that reverberates like deep thunder in the ears is the 'rumbling' (stanita). Taking of deep breaths is 'sighing' (svasita). Weeping is called the 'crying' (rudita). (24-25).

'Sit' sounds are to be made at the end of sexual inter-course. The 'phut' sound (phutkrta) and the groaning (kujita) are regional varieties of 'sit'. (26).

The deep throaty sound of mating peacocks is called the groaning by some. Other scholars say that 'phut' sound is only another variety of groaning. (27).

The noise produced at the splitting of a bamboo stick is known as the 'phut' sound. Alternately, some say that the repetitious sound produced by pipal (Ficus religiosa) berries falling into water is the guttural 'phut' sound. Others say that 'phut' is an inarticulate murmuring. (28-29)

'Jiya' and 'Oh! mother' are calling out for mother sounds (ambartha). Words such as 'Oh! stop' are uttered to prohibit (nisedhartha) more pain. 'Enough' or 'that is enough' are also

pleadings to stop (alam-artha). 'Let me go', 'free me' express a desire to be freed (moksartha). 'Kill me', 'destroy me' are words of painful joy. 'I am dying, help me' are cries for compassion (karunokti). (30-32).

Unclear and restless words signify affection and love (snigdhokti). 'Oh! you so and so' are rude words (parusokti). (33)

Continuous guttural crow-like sounds are called the crying of crows (kakaruta). (34).

The sucking sound that is produced in the mouth of those addicted to strong spices or those who do a lot of loud singing is the 'sit' sound of love. (35).

Cries of ducks and other birds can be made at the end of sexual intercourse. These express the passions created by sexual excitement. (36).

These are some of the external signs of a sexually aroused woman: she has goose-flesh all over her body; her limbs become limp; she closes her eyes; there is sweat on her cheeks; her genital area becomes moist; she makes incoherent guttural sounds of passion; she shakes her hands; she gets agitated if her love tries to leave; she kicks and pulls her lover back. (37-40).

A woman's love increases when reciprocated by a man. According to the great sage there are four forms of love. Love born by intimacy (abhyasiki-priti), love through fantasy (abhimaniki-priti), love by resemblance (sampratyaya-priti) and love for physical pleasure (vaisayiki-priti). (41-42).

The love that develops from being together on hunting expeditions, art exhibitions, dance and music recitals is the love by intimacy (abhyasiki-priti). (43).

The love that is born spontaneously, without previous association, friendship or intention is the love by fantasy (abhimaniki-priti). (44).

Love through resemblance (sampratyaya-priti) happens when a lover is reminded of his beloved because of some

likeness in the fellatio done to him either by an eunuch or a courtesan. (45-46a).

Love for some selfish reason is the love for physical pleasure (vaisayiki-priti). (46b).

I have explained the forms of love. Now to discuss regional characteristics. (47a).

A cultured lover should do only that which is agreeable to local custom. Women of the middle country do not like nail marking and kissing. Women of Bahlika and Avanti regions are of very high moral character and do not go in for foreplay and kissing. They prefer imaginative coitus postures. However, though they do not like nail marking they like to be given love blows. Those born in the Abhira region love to be embraced. Women of Malava like to be kissed. (47b-50).

Middle country or Madhya-desa is the area that lies between the Himalayas and the Vindhya ranges, situated to the west of Prayaga (Allahabad) and east of Vinasana (Harayana).

Bahlika is the same as Bactria and is situated in Afghanistan, south of the river Oxus.

Avanti is the ancient name for Ujjain.

Abhira refers to a tribe that is said to have lived in north-west India. According to the *Brahmanda-purana* (Ch. IV), the river Indus flowed through the Abhira country. Later, the Abhiras spread to many other parts of India.

Malava was originally the name of a people who lived in the lower Ravi region. The Greek historians called them 'Malloi'. The Malavas later settled in the western parts of present Madhya Pradesh giving their name to the region.

Women born in the valleys of the Candrabhaga (Chenab), Tungabhadra, Sarayu (Gogra), Sindhu (Indus), Iravati (Ravi) and Vitasta (Jhelum) rivers cannot be pleased without oral sex. They also like gentle love blows, bites and nail marks. (51-52).

Delicate women of the Lata country love to be embraced. They dance with joy and become very wet with vaginal secre-

tions at the prospect of coitus. (53).

Lata is Gujarat of today, south of the river Mahi.

Women of Avanti are also dainty but love sexual intercourse. Women of Andhra and Purandhra are sinful, shameless and given to many bad habits. They love sex and are expert in 'mare's coitus'. (54b-55a).

Andhra is the region between the rivers Godavari and Krishna. It falls within the boundaries of the present Andhra Pradesh.

Purandhra or Pundra probably denotes northern Bengal.

Mare's coitus (vadavakarana) is the mare's posture where the woman forcefully holds the penis with the help of the vaginal muscles. This is possible only after a lot of training and practice.

Women of the female-kingdom (stri-rajya) and Kosala have a tremendous itch in their vaginas. They can only get sexually aroused with rough play or when ravished with large artificial penises. (55b-56).

Vicitra Goyutha

Adbhutalingodbhava

Stri-rajya or female-kingdom is frequently mentioned in Puranic literature but is difficult to locate geographically. According to the *Skanda-purana* (I, ii, 39, 153), stri-rajya was one of the five major regions of India and had 500,000 villages. The *Garuda-purana* (I, 55, 15) places it in the area around the Indus valley, modern Mathura and the Vindhya ranges.

Kosala is the region around modern Ayodhya along the banks of the Sarayu (Gogra) river.

The women of Maharastra are vulgar, without shame and talk rudely. They generally know all the sixty-four arts but reach orgasm very quickly. These characteristics are also true of the women of Pataliputra. But they are very secretive about it. (57-58a).

Maharastra roughly coincides with the modern west Indian state of the same name.

Pataliputra is the ancient name for the region around modern Patna in Bihar.

Women of the Dravida country like to be stroked all over and secrete a lot of vaginal fluid when aroused. They are accomplished in making love, true to their word and good at sweet talk. They like oral sex. (58b-60a).

Dravida country is India south of the river Godavari.

Women of the forest dwellers (Vanavasika) are tolerant and of moderate passion. But they make cruel selfish jokes. They are clever at laughing at the faults and defects of others but hiding their own. They cannot be trusted. (60b-61).

Vanavasika refers to the south-western region known today as Kerala.

Women belonging to the Gauda and Banga region have very soft limbs, enjoy sweet words and love to be embraced and kissed. They are not very passionate and are devoid of bad habits. (62-63a).

Gauda is central Bengal and Banga is the ancient name for south-east Bengal.

A mere touch is enough for the women of Kamarupa to become excited and wet with vaginal fluids. Their bodies are as soft as mimosa flowers and they like to hear pleasant words. (63b-64).

Kamarupa is modern Assam and probably Manipur in eastern India.

The shameless women of Kalinga delight in all manners of nail marking and are ever ready for sex. They respond quickly to stimulation of their clitoris and oral sex. They even like to be beaten. (65-66a).

Kalinga is the coastal region between the Mahanadi and Godavari rivers and includes the modern eastern state of Orissa (Awasthi, 1992).

For characteristics of women of regions not mentioned here one should be guided by experience and reasoning. (66b).

Now to define the nature of a woman who is in love and ready for the battle of passion. (67).

Delight, joy, enthusiasm and amazement at the thought of sexual union. Sweating, goose-flesh, hoarse voice, pale skin, trembling body, blushing at the thought of sex and memory loss. These are all the outer signs of men and women in love. (68-69).

I shall describe, to the best of my knowledge, more symptoms of a woman in love. She is delighted to see her lover approaching. When he comes near her she murmurs words such as 'Oh! how happy I am' to her self. She eulogizes her lover in the presence of her friends. She lies on a bed facing him ready to worship his every command. She wakes up before him. She treats his enemies as her enemies and is pained at his loss. She donates her own wealth and embraces him with love. She considers his wealth as her own and protects it with her life. His happiness is her happiness and his pain is her pain. She looks upon him with respect. She is always ready to please him with sex. She tells him all her secrets. Her very existence is a symbol of her love. She hides her faults from him in the hope that he will always love her and asks for no reward. She kisses and embraces him while he sleeps without expecting any response. If she ever sees him preoccupied she thinks that he is having an affair with someone else. She even suspects her own love marks to be of another woman. She is overjoyed if he reciprocates even a little of her love. She catches hold of his hands and places them on her eyes and cheeks. Remembering her love play with him she becomes emotional. When he returns from a long journey she kisses him again and again. She finds some excuse to be near him. These are all the signs of a woman in love. A man in love behaves in more or less the same manner. The conduct of a woman who dislikes her man is just the opposite. (70-82).

Thus ends the seventh chapter on all matters connected with sex in the work called 'Rati-ratna-pradipika' by King Devaraja the Elder. Here ends the work called 'Rati-ratna-pradipika'.

Adarsadarsana

THE ARTIST

The illustrations that accompany this translation of the *Rati-ratna-pradipika* are—unless otherwise stated—the work of 'Ganjifa'[1] Raghupati Bhatta.

Raghupati Bhatta was born in 1957 at a small village called Belmannu (Karkala taluk). This little village is situated in the fertile and tropical south-western coastal district of South Kanara (Dakshina Kannada), not far from the port city of Mangalore and the temple town of Udupi which attracts thousands of devout pilgrims each year to its famous Krsna temple. Raghupati was the sixth in a family of four sons and three daughters. His father, Anantarama Bhatta, was very closely associated with the famous Vaisnava monasteries of Sode and Puttige and his mother, Krsnaveni, was a devotee of Sri Krsna.

At the age of seven Raghupati's father suggested that he join a school in Nagamangala (Mandya district) and live with his sister for the period of his education. Nagamangala is an ancient town, about 70 kilometres north-west of Mysore. The town and its surrounding countryside is dotted with temples and sculptured relics belonging to the medieval (11th and 12th centuries A.D.) Hoysala period. Young Raghupati was fascinated by them. The ornate sculptured representations of gods, goddesses and voluptuous heavenly nymphs (apsaras) made a very deep impression on his artistic mind. All his spare time after school hours was spent looking at them, studying them and trying to translate their likeness on to paper. More than the sculptures, the murals in the Saumya Kesavasvami temple in the centre of the town impressed him the most. He instinctively knew what course his life would take and what profession he would follow. Deep down he had made up his mind to become an artist.

In 1977 he finished his final year in school. As his father was now in Bangalore Raghupati decided to go there. The open and liberated atmosphere of this large metropolis offered freedom and the opportunity to meet new people. Raghupati made the most of this. One day he happened to visit the Chitrakala Parishat, an art school that was patronized by the famous Russian artist D.S. Roerich, his actress wife Devika Rani and members of the Mysore royal family. It was guided by the great visionary and artist Sri M.S. Nanjunda Rao. Raghupati Bhatta spent most of 1977 learning, informally, the basics of drawing and painting. As Nanjunda Rao has devoted his life to the revival and propagation of traditional Mysore or Karnataka style he naturally encouraged Raghupati to understand and recreate this style.

At first Raghupati found inspiration in the traditional style of painting. The delicate and flowing lines, bright intense colours, decorative compositions and fine workmanship of the 'chadda' playing cards of the Mummadi Krsnaraja period (1794-1868 A.D.) attracted him the most. He therefore started specializing in this genre.

After his initial training he went back to Nagamangala of his school days and set up a small studio. Here he studied, experimented and evolved. At first he recreated the delicate work of 19th century playing cards. He painted hieratic poses of gods and goddesses, royal portraits, mystical yantras, esoteric symbols and narratives from the *Ramayana* epic. He experimented with organic and mineral pigments. He learnt to make his own brushes from soft squirrel hair. But, as he became more and more proficient in the 'ganjifa' style, he felt the need to move on. He needed more feedback from other artists and scholars who could both guide and criticize him. He needed to see the work of other artists both traditional and contemporary.

So he decided to move to a place that would expose his work to a larger number of viewers. Nagamangala was too small and out-of-the-way place for this. Bangalore was out of the question now as he could not afford to live in a city that was fast becoming the most expensive place in India. Mysore was his next choice, but that too was beyond his immediate means. So he selected the small fortified town of Srirangapattana, medieval seat of the Wadiyar dynasty and the famous capital of Tipu Sultan. It was affordable and at the same time, being on the highway between Bangalore and Mysore, was visited by a large number of people. Tourists from all over the world came here to see the historical monuments. Pilgrims from all parts of India came here to offer prayers at the ancient temple of Ranganathasvami, a form of Lord Visnu.

By now Raghupati Bhatta was married and had a family to support. To make both ends meet he started a small 'ganjifa' art school. For a nominal fee he taught young artists the art and craft on which he had spent so many formative years of his life. Gradually, the idea of a 'Ganjifa' museum took root in his mind. If there was such a museum he could not only exhibit his growing collection of old historical playing cards but also his own and his students' work. With great effort and sincere dedication, his dream became a reality on 26th March 1991. He managed to get a place near the ancient Ranganathasvami temple to start his small, but well planned, 'Ganjifa' art gallery. Significantly, Raghupati Bhatta chose the small surviving pavilion where two centuries before, in 1794, King Mummadi Krsnaraja Wadiyar—the greatest innovator of the Mysore ganjifa—was born. This little gallery, which houses 'ganjifa' cards from all over India, still attracts a lot of visitors. It has now become a monument, not only to the artistic talent of Raghupati Bhatta but also to the memory of Mummadi Krsnaraja Wadiyar, the artist-scholar king of Mysore. More recently Raghupati has moved to Mysore and hopes that he will be able to have another 'Ganjifa' gallery here as well.

The sets of playing cards that Raghupati Bhatta painted during the early period of his development were technically and stylistically exact replicas of early cards. But faithful duplication of the work of early artists was not for Raghupati. He was searching for a more creative and individual idiom using the small format of traditional playing cards. At first his innovations were limited to changes in compositions and colour combinations. He painted traditional subjects but added details, such as costume designs and thin long figures, that were not found in old playing cards. Gradually he introduced scenic elements that were unknown to the traditional idiom of plain monochrome backgrounds. Raghupati felt that if he could somehow reduce the decorative and emphasize the symbolic-narrative quality of traditional playing card images he could take a significant step forward. He could then express his own creativity through the medium of an ancient art form.

This is exactly what he has been doing recently. Some of his playing cards, based on the *Ramayana* narrative that he painted in 1993 and 1994, use traditional images in a new form. For instance he retains the traditional symbols of Rama as an ideal king and Sita as a devoted wife, but their forms are no longer idealized and deified. They are simple and human, set against a dream-like landscape. The erotic sets of Raghupati Bhatta are also innovative. Along with his tall and simplified human figures he adds many diverse traditional elements: full round breasts and thin hips of Hoysala sculptures, fine outline from traditional playing cards and large almond eyes from Karnataka folk puppets.

In his most recent work, Raghupati has gone beyond using diverse elements as separate motifs. All elements have fused to form images that are both dream-like and earthy at the same time. Part of the figures that people his cards seem to melt away into the background, while their solid torsos, made of gesso relief work, give them a stability and bulk that is quite tangible. And yet they are clear images that narrate a traditional tale using an ancient symbolic language. His most recent (1995-1996) series of *Durga-saptasati* paintings are based accurately on traditional art manuals such as the *Visnudharmottara purana* (6th century A.D.) and the Tantras and yet they visually go beyond all tradition. They are probably the most mature and creative works of Raghupati Bhatta.

Though Raghupati Bhatta has developed a style and visual language that is his own, he still uses the old technique[2] for making his cards and painting them with mineral and vegetable pigments that are still available in the Indian market.

He has had two very successful exhibitions in London in 1992 and 1994. He had a one-man show at the London centre of the Bharatiya Vidya Bhavan. Then he participated in the Oxford Art in Action workshop where he demonstrated his technique and recent work. The Victoria and Albert Museum, London, commissioned him to make 60 cards of the *Ramayana* series which now form a part of their permanent collection. At home he has won the Mysore Dasara Award (1988), the Kamaladevi Chattopadhyaya 'Visvakarma' Award (1989), Jaycee State (1991) and National (1992) Awards, the President of India National Award (1993) and the twenty-sixth annual Karnataka Lalitakala Academy Award (1996).

Raghupati Bhatta has recently been exposed to Western art. Perhaps in the future this may have a beneficial effect on his visual language. But at the moment his style remains both unique and characteristic of his artistic personality. He has become so identified with his style that the word 'Ganjifa' has become a part of his name. He is now known as Ganjifa Raghupati Bhatta.

NOTES

1. Indian traditional playing cards are generally known as 'Ganjifa' (or Kanjifa) and this same word has been used in Nepal, Iran, some Arab countries and Turkey. The first use of this word is found in a work of 1399 A.D. known as 'Annals of Egypt and Syria' by Yusuf ibn Thaghri-Birdi. It relates a story of a Mamluk Amir called al Malik al Muayyad, who purchased a slave boy for

2000 dirhams that he had won in a game of 'kanjifa' cards. The word is most probably derived from the Persian 'ganj' meaning treasure or hoard though some scholars are of the opinion that the term may be of Turkish origin. The more ancient Sanskrit name for playing cards is 'krida-patra' (lit. play-leaves).

2. Traditional playing cards are made from several layers of paper pasted together, or from pieces of cotton cloth stuck on to layered paper. When cotton cloth is used it is primed with rice gruel (ganji) and covered with a layer of white earth. The mineral and vegetable pigments used to paint the designs are generally mixed with animal glue (mara-vajra), though occasionally gum arabic is substituted for glue.

BIBLIOGRAPHY

ABHYANKAR, Kashinath Vasudev & J.M. Shukla. 1986. *A Dictionary of Sanskrit Grammar,* Baroda: Oriental Institute.

AWASTHI, A.B.L. 1992. *Purana Index,* New Delhi: Navarang.

COMFORT, Alex. 1965. *The Koka Shastra and Other Medieval Writings on Love,* New York: Stein & Day.

DANIELOU, Alain. 1994. *The Complete Kama Sutra,* Rochester: Inner Traditions.

DE, Sushil Kumar. 1969. *Ancient Indian Erotics and Erotic Literature,* Calcutta: Firma K.L. Mukhopadhyay.

EVOLA, Julius. 1983. *The Metaphysics of Sex,* London: East-West Publications.

GREGERSEN, Edgar. 1982. *Sexual Practices. The Story of Human Sexuality,* London: Mitchell Beazley.

GULVADI, Shantoshkumar. 1994. *Ganjipha Kale* (in Kannada), Bangalore: Karnataka Lalitakala Academy.

IYENGAR, Pandita K. Rangaswami (Ed.). 1922. *Ratiratnapradipika of Praudha Devaraja Maharaja,* Mysore: Jayamangala Press.

LI, Zhisui. 1996. *The Private Life of Chairman Mao,* London: Arrow Books.

RAO, C. Hayavadana. 1943. *History of Mysore (1399-1799),* Vol. I, Bangalore: Government Press.

RAO, S.K. Ramachandra. 1989. *Pratima Kosha,* Vol. II, Madras: Giri Trading Agency.

RAY, Tridibnath. 1964. *Kalyana Malla's Ananga Ranga,* New York: The Citadel Press.

SHELDON, W., C.W. Dupertuis & E. McDermott. 1954. *Atlas of Man: A Guide for Somatotyping of the Adult Male at All Ages,* New York: Harper.

TRIMMER, Dr. Eric J. (Editor-in-Chief). 1978. *The Visual Dictionary of Sex,* London: Pan Books.

UPADHYAYA, S.C. 1965. *Rati Rahasya of Pandit Kokkoka,* Bombay: D.B. Taraporevala Sons & Co. Pvt. Ltd.

WALKER, Benjamin. 1977. *Encyclopedia of Esoteric Man,* London: Routledge & Kegan Paul.

WARD, Brian. 1984. *Sex and Life (Guideline Series),* London: Macdonald & Co. Ltd.

INDEX